I Can't Even Walk

Without You Holding My Hand

Justin Fisher

Cover design by Nathan Crocker (www.powerfulart.com)

I Can't Even Walk (Without You Holding My Hand)
c – 2011 by Justin Fisher

Library of Congress Cataloging-in-Publication Data

Fisher, Justin
        I can't even walk.

ISBN-13: 978-1456405137
ISBN-10: 1456405136

To the Amazing Kelly, Buddy Roe, and Ladybug.
I am so incredibly blessed
to be able to call you my family.

Not to us, O LORD,
not to us but to your name be the glory,
because of your love and faithfulness.

Psalm 115:1

Now therefore, I pray You, if I have found favor in
Your sight, let me know Your ways that I may know
You, so that I may find favor in Your sight.

Exodus 33:13a(NASB)

Table of Contents

<u>*ACKNOWLEDGMENTS*</u>

My sincerest thanks to:

David – your encouragement and advice might not have made this possible, but certainly more probable than before.

My editorial review board: **Dianna Hyde, Liesl Ward, Tommy Battles and Saint Green.** I simply could not have done this without you.

Nathan Crocker – your creative expertise never ceases to amaze me. Go Dawgs!

Kelly – If I tried to fill every page of this book with my thoughts of and thanks toward you, it could not contain them all.

Preface

This book is not about me. This book is about the infinite love, and grace, and mercy that the God of the universe lavished upon us when, instead of demanding justice, He offered the gift of His only Son, who suffered and died on the Cross as the only acceptable sacrifice for our sins. This book was written to bring Him praise, and honor, and glory (Ephesians 1:14).

I do, however, think that it is incumbent upon me, the author, to tell you a bit about myself so that you, the reader, will have at least some frame of reference. I was born on August 11th, 1973, in the old Laird Hospital building in Union, Mississippi. That is a short, simple sentence, but it says quite a bit about me. To explain, I'll start at the end of the sentence and work my way backwards.

I am a Mississippian and proud of it. I graduated from Mississippi State University with two degrees, and I am proud of those accomplishments. Now, some of you are probably already thinking, "People from Mississippi can't even *read*!" Well, yes, we can read. Some of us can even write. Folks like John Grisham, Eudora Welty, William Faulkner, and Tennessee Williams are all from Mississippi. Let me pause here to say that I have no delusions of grandeur, and I in no way am comparing my writings to theirs. There is, however, something about the South in general, and Mississippi in particular, that makes people here good storytellers. And that's what I do. I tell stories. I see myself as a raconteur. Jerry Clower (there's another great Mississippi storyteller) often said, "I don't tell funny stories, I just tell stories funny." That basically sums up the way I recount events as well.

I was born in Union, Mississippi. It's a small town with a population of approximately 2,000 located in the East-Central portion of the state. I was raised, however, ten miles away at Route 1, Box 104, Conehatta, Mississippi. "Conehatta" is a Choctaw Indian word that means "dirty skunk."

There is some discrepancy as to the manner in which the area came to have its name. I have always claimed that "dirty skunk" was probably what the Native Americans called the white people who took their land. My uncle, however, says that it is simply because of an abundance of the worthless varmints.

Whatever the case, when one's formative years are spent in a place called Dirty Skunk, there's only one place to go, and that's up. Talk about being born under a bad sign! People often ask me, "What's it close to?" My reply is, "Nothing." The interstate exit signs in this area have names like Chunky, Lake, Forrest, and Sebastopol printed on them. The nearest village of any size, Meridian, is about 45 miles away. The only reason anyone might know the name "Meridian" is that it is located right off Interstate 20, and they might have passed through there going somewhere else.

I was born in the Old Laird Hospital building. A prominent physician in town was Doctor Earl Laird, after whom the hospital and one of my aunts is named. As the phrase "the Old Laird Hospital" would imply, there is now a New Laird Hospital, out on the Highway 15 bypass. The rest of the world might think that the town of Union has indeed been "bypassed"; and while it is true that not much has changed, I still call it home.

My birth year is 1973. That may, in the long run, may be the most integral part of the telling of this story. I am convinced that had I been born twenty, or maybe even as little as ten, years later, I would not have had the opportunity to deal with many of the challenges in my life. You see, I was born with the condition cerebral palsy, commonly known as CP.

I use an electric wheelchair for mobility, so lots of folks assume I'm paralyzed from the waist down. This is not the case. I have full feeling in all my extremities. CP, however, presents its own set of complications. When I was born, the

3

oxygen was cut off to the part of my brain that works the muscles. In 1973, sonograms were not available to show complications during pregnancy and delivery. Had I been born several years later, Mom would have probably had a C-section; and I in all likelihood would have turned out "normal."

Because of my cerebral palsy, my balance and coordination are severely affected, and all of my movements are almost in slow motion. It's like I have to think to tell my leg, "Move this way." Sometimes they respond well, and other times, not so well. Sometimes the same messages are sent to several muscle groups when I only need one set to respond. Telling my hands to grip tighter on a can opener may result in my legs stiffening, or flexing my calf muscles might cause my teeth and jaws to clench tightly shut. It's a little like a short circuit in the wiring between my brain and muscles.

God has blessed me with this condition. That's right, I said blessed. In order to accept the gift God has offered, we must admit that we are utterly helpless to save ourselves. That means abandoning our pride and admitting we're scum and trash (Isaiah 64:6) when compared to the holiness of God. Cerebral palsy has helped me in that pursuit. It has helped teach me humility, and patience, and trust in the One who is greater than me.

Not Religion, Relationship

Baggage Claim

Relationships are tough. No two ways about it. And the nature of the relationship doesn't seem to matter. They all have their difficulties. Parents and children, co-workers, sweethearts, employees and employers, spouses, church goers, club members; all of them with their own set of struggles to deal with … or run from. My pastor reminds the congregation that even this whole "God thing" is not about a religion but about a relationship.

Do you know what makes relationships tough? Baggage. That's the stuff that we all bring to the table in a relationship. Yes, all of us have baggage. Battle scars from relationships gone bad. Bruises from past struggles. Hang-ups because of previous traumas. Habits and personality quirks that some find endearing and others find extremely annoying. Now, some people have more baggage than others, both in quantity and quality; but the fact remains that even those people you think are perfect, or lead storybook lives, have baggage.

Allow me to tell you a little about my own baggage. As stated in the preface, I was born with cerebral palsy, and I use a wheelchair as my main means of mobility. Those who know and love me might say that this isn't baggage. But it is. Anyone who meets me must, within the first thirty seconds of our relationship, deal with a multitude of logistical and social issues that they may never have thought about before. They may even have to deal with their own baggage or perceptions they have about people with disabilities from a cultural standpoint.

Most people have become adept at hiding their baggage. For example, if you've got a tattoo of Elmer Fudd on your lower back that you obtained during a drunken midnight frolic, or if your father's an alcoholic and dresses in a pink tutu when there's a full moon, or if you went on Oprah to talk about the Neo-Nazi space alien abductors that forced you to go on some strange weight loss program and you don't want to divulge such things to people you meet, you can probably keep those things hidden if you try hard enough, at least during an initial conversation.

I don't have that luxury. Most of my baggage is already out there, up front, for everybody to see – and not only to see, but to deal with immediately. It's like telling someone your whole life's story, scars and all, on the first date. And speaking of dating, dealing with my disability was compounded a thousand times during my single days when it came to relationships with members of the opposite sex. I felt sometimes like I was wearing a flashing neon sign that said, "Look at everything you'll have to deal with if you go out with this person!"

This leads me to confess that I have baggage about my baggage. Truth be known, people in general probably deal with my disability better than I expect them to. However, when it came to dating or romantic relationships, I was really self-conscious about how I looked around the opposite sex, especially if I had to do anything physical. From taking a heavy book down from a shelf to walking on my crutches from point A to point B, from buckling a seatbelt to transferring from my wheelchair to a movie theatre seat, I always felt like I was exposing every weakness. And we all know the last thing a man wants to show, or a woman wants to see, is weakness.

Many moons ago, before Kelly and I were married, I dated some. After a particularly discouraging date, I felt like I'd been kicked in the gut. The conversation I had with myself went something like this, "Way to go loser! You really sealed that deal. She'll never want to be in the same room with you again."

Later that night, however, after I'd come to my senses, I realized three things that we all might do well to learn from when it comes to our identity in Christ. First, I am who I am; God made me like this and no amount of fretting will ever change that. In fact, my disability is meant to bring glory to God. Notice in 2 Corinthians 12:7-10, Paul writes, "To keep me from becoming conceited … there was given me *a thorn in my flesh*.... Three times I pleaded with the Lord to take it away from me. But he said to me, '*My grace is sufficient for you, for my power is made perfect in weakness.*' Therefore *I will boast all the more gladly about my weaknesses*, so that Christ's power may rest on me. That is why, for Christ's sake, *I delight in weaknesses*, in insults, in hardships, in persecutions, in difficulties. *For when I am weak, then I am strong"(emphasis added).*

Second, I realized that any woman who falls in love with me will love me, not just in spite of the CP, but maybe *because* of it. She'll realize that having a disability has, at least in part, made me who I am. The apostle John tells us in chapter 9, verses 1-3, "As (Jesus) went along, he saw a man blind from birth. His disciples asked him, 'Rabbi, who sinned, this man or his parents, that he was born blind?' 'Neither this man nor his parents sinned,' said Jesus, 'but *this happened so that the work of God might be displayed in his life'"* *(emphasis added).*

Then third, and probably most importantly, I remembered 2 Corinthians 3:5, which says, "Not that we are competent in ourselves to claim anything for ourselves, but *our competence comes from God*" *(emphasis added).* Our sufficiency, any sufficiency, or ability or capability that we have, comes from God. No one is perfect. My date was human, just like me. Formed by the same Creator. And carrying baggage. I realized then and there that anyone I would ever go out with would have baggage, too. It would just take me longer to see her baggage than it would for her to see mine. From that point on, anytime I thought I had met "the perfect woman," I would begin to get nervous and start asking questions. "What if she's got a tattoo of Elmer Fudd on her lower back? What if her father dresses up in a pink tutu when there's a full moon? Or worse, what if she's got relatives that are Ole Miss fans?

What's in a Name?

For thirty some odd years, my Dad worked a blue-collar factory job at U.S. Electrical Motors in Philadelphia, Mississippi. As a child growing up, I loved hearing stories about the goings on at the "Motor Mill." I think maybe more entertaining than the stories themselves were the names of the characters in the stories. Dad worked with men called Goat, Squat Rock, Bear (incidentally Bear was Hot Triplet's son), Punk, Tater, Bummer and Tiny. I never experienced a "take your child to work" day, so the only character I ever met was Tiny. Tiny weighed close to two hundred fifty pounds, so I could only imagine what the rest of these men really looked like. As the character attributes and legends grew and developed in my mind, I came to *love* nicknames.

I even love my nickname. My whole immediate family and most of my extended family call me Shug. Dad gave me my nickname. That's one of the reasons I like it so much. Where did my Dad come up with such a name? Here's the story I was told. On the 1960's sitcom "The Beverly Hillbillies," there was a recurring character named Shorty. Shorty was not a regular, but he did occasionally make appearances. When he did show up, one of his main objectives was to flirt with the secretary at Mr. Drysdale's bank.

Shorty's stage name was Shug Fisher. My Dad thought that was a great name and, after all, our last name is Fisher, so it just fit. The "flirting with secretaries" part also fit. I guess you could call it a self-fulfilling prophecy.

I never remember my Dad calling me Justin. My mom says that when they brought me home from the hospital, Dad held me down for the dog to see and smell of and said, "Here's Shug." I remember once, when Mom and Dad came to pick me up from summer camp, Dad said to my counselor, "Thanks for taking care of Shug." "Who?" my counselor asked. Dad could not think of my real name. We might still be at the Henry S. Jacobs Campground today if Mom hadn't been there to help him remember.

My life has been filled with great people with great nicknames. One of my favorite Sunday school teachers was Squirrel. Scooter and Rooster were both in my wedding. My nieces are Sweetpea, Peanut, and Jellybean. Cash was an assistant to me as evening coordinator at Jefferson State Community College, a.k.a. Jeffy Tech. My best friend has several nicknames, including Hambone and Rabbit. Other friends include Super K, D-Mo, Moose, Barney, Thorndog, Jo-Bo, Spanky, Skip, and of course, Bubba.

Some of these names are spin-offs from these people's given names. Most, however, are derived from an event they were involved in or a character trait they posses. This brings me to one of my favorite nicknames of all time, Barnabas. Acts 4:36-37 says, "Joseph, a Levite from Cyprus, whom the apostles called Barnabas (which means Son of Encouragement), sold a field he owned and brought the money and put it at the apostles' feet." "Son of Encouragement" is a great nickname. Notice that in the verse his name was not Barnabas. His name was Joseph. The apostles gave him this nickname. I do not believe that this nickname was a self-fulfilling prophecy as mine was. I believe Joseph did something very special to earn this title. Let's back up a few verses.

Verse thirty-four tells us, "There were no needy persons among them. For from time to time those who owned lands or houses sold them, brought the money from the sales." So we know that this selling and giving was not an unusual thing. This verse makes it seem a common practice. So why single out Joseph? Why this special nickname, Son of Encouragement? Well, if you read the entire book of Acts, over and over again we see Barnabas encouraging others. In Chapter, nine we see him bringing Saul into the company and fellowship of other believers after his conversion experience on the Damascus Road. We see evidence in Chapter 11 when, after hearing of the grace of God impacting the Greeks, he travels to Antioch and encourages the new believers to "remain true to the Lord with all their hearts." Verse twenty-four of this chapter says, "He was a good man, full of the Holy Spirit and faith…" In Chapter thirteen the Holy Spirit sets him apart for a special work in Cyprus. Acts 14:3 reads, "So Paul and Barnabas spent considerable time [in Iconium], speaking boldly for the Lord, who confirmed the message of his grace by enabling them to do miraculous signs and wonders."

Many times in the Bible, writers refer to their converts as "sons." Joseph was most likely a convert of Luke and was called Barnabas because he encouraged all those around him. I would to God that we would all get the nickname Barnabas. I pray that we would be an encouragement to everyone we meet and leave the world a better place from having been here.

The Fish, the Rabbit, and the Deer

My best friend is named Justin Peters. Yes, another Justin. Our name, however, is just the beginning of our similarities. We were both born in 1973 in Mississippi, both have cerebral palsy, and both graduated with Economics degrees from Mississippi State University. We roomed together at State, but we'd known each other virtually our whole lives before that.

Justin and I met at what was then called the Mississippi Crippled Children's Center when we were two years old. (That would now be a very politically incorrect title, so several years ago the name of the institution was changed.) Our story really began on a Sunday when our respective parents met in the lobby to pick us up from the Center for the standard once-a-week visit. One of us said, "Bye, Justin!" and the other one said, "Bye, Justin!" and our parents freaked out. What an amazing number of similarities! This was the beginning of a lifelong friendship.

Justin and I lived on opposite sides of the state. He lived in Vicksburg, which is on the Mississippi River just across the state line from Louisiana. I lived near Meridian, which is very near the Alabama state line. Growing up, however, we saw each other two or three times a year, during summer, Christmas, or Spring breaks.

We grew up together. No, we didn't live across the street or see each other every day at school, but we helped each other grow. Imagine having a disability that affects every aspect of your life. Now imagine having a best friend that is the same age that has the same disability to go through it with you. The task somehow doesn't seem quite as daunting, does it?

Justin and I love the singing country comedian Ray Stephens. Stephens recorded a song called "Vacation Bible School." It's about the antics that ensue when he spikes the student preacher's lemonade with moonshine on a particularly hot and dusty Sunday. Stephens concludes that song by saying something like, "Well, I gotta go now friends, but one day you'll have to get me to tell you about the time me and Arlo Wiggins put an electric eel in the baptismal pool. That preacher had no more than put his big toe in there, when he commenced to walking on the water! It was down-right inspirational." It just leaves the listener wanting more.

In the same way, I feel I could fill volumes of books with stories about our crazy times together, and each one would just lead to the next. Even as both of us turn thirty-seven, the "Adventures of Justin and Justin" are still being written. This last sentence reminds me that having two Justins around can be a bit confusing. Imagine

17

a new acquaintance calling our dorm room at State:

Caller:	May I speak to Justin please?
Justin:	Which one?
Caller:	The one in the wheelchair?
Justin:	Which one?
Caller:	The Economics major?
Justin:	Which one?
Caller:	The Delta Chi (We also pledged together.)
Justin:	Which one?

Early on, to eliminate some of the confusion, our parents took to calling us by an abbreviated form of our last names. Since I am Justin Fisher, I was called "Fish" and, in like manner, Justin Peters was called "Pete". My nickname stuck, but Pete's went through many evolutions. On Pete's motorized wheelchair/scooter, his main mode of transportation, there was a speed control knob. On the slowest setting was a picture of a turtle and on the fastest, a picture of a rabbit. A friend noticed that Pete always went around in "rabbit mode" and also noticed that, ironically, this was in stark contrast to the speed at which he went when he was *not* using his scooter. So Justin Peter's nickname became Peter Rabbit, and eventually it was shortened simply to Rabbit.

So now we have the "Fish" and the "Rabbit" from my title, but where does the deer come it? Well, several years after we graduated, we met back in Starkville to spend the night at a friend's house and go deer hunting. The Oktibbeha Wildlife Refuge is located just outside of the city limits, and this sanctuary has handicapped accessible hunting blinds. We made the appropriate reservations and went hunting on a Friday afternoon. I shot at and missed a doe that came out when it was almost too dark to see. Rabbit and I felt like our luck as deer slayers would be better the next morning.

As we set out Saturday before dawn, the drive out to the refuge was foggy, like driving in pea soup. Rabbit and I were talking and carrying on as usual when something caught my attention out of the corner of my eye. In an instant a brown blur smashed into the driver's side headlight and door panel. We had been hit by a kamikaze deer! (I will never for the life of me understand this insanity! These same elusive creatures that you must sit in the cold woods wearing camouflage for hours in silence just to catch a glimpse of will somehow magically appear roadside when they hear an automobile engine and see bright lights! And as if that were not crazy enough, you don't even need a gun to kill them! They just thrust themselves headlong into your vehicle, like a Japanese fighter pilot at Pearl Harbor.)

We found a spot to pull the van over, and there was only minor cosmetic damage. Rabbit and I were now in a dilemma. Do we try to retrieve the deer that is most certainly dead, judging by the force with which she was hit, or do we go on to our hunting spot? We both know that a bird (or deer) in the hand is worth two in the bush, so we elected for the former.   We drove back to the spot where we hit the deer, and she was indeed laying on the road bank, dead as a hammer.

Rabbit and I both use forearm crutches to help with our balance when walking. Balance, however, was not an easy feat by itself on this steep roadside bank, not to mention the difficulty of being physically challenged and trying to drag a deer carcass up an incline. "Why not go get help?" you might ask. Well, it was an adventure, and, if successful, it would be an accomplishment. You see, for an able bodied hunter, bagging and retrieving game is usually no big deal. But Rabbit and I had always had to rely on someone else to drag the animal after we had made a kill on any other hunting trip. This was our chance to do both. It was our chance at being "normal."

After considerable effort, we dragged the deer to the top of the bank. Try as we might, though, we could not lift her up into the back of my mini-van. After many failed attempts, we decided the most obvious solution was to drag the carcass onto the modified wheelchair lift. We decided it would be easier to move the van than the deer. I climbed into the driver's seat to reposition the vehicle. In the commotion of the situation, I could not get my bearings. Both my rear doors were open, so the line of sight was obstructed out of my side-view mirrors. Also, Justin was not quite tall enough to be seen through the rearview mirror over the back seat.

Now, I didn't want to run over the Rabbit or the deer; so I yelled for Justin to raise one of his crutches high in the air so that I could see where he was. About this time the sun has come up, and I heard the distant sound of a vehicle approaching. I want you to picture in your mind the scene this car is about to pass. A mini-van is parked on the shoulder of the road with a wheelchair lift extended from the sliding side door. One crippled man is trying to drag a dead deer onto a wheelchair lift, while another is balancing on one crutch and holding the other straight up in the air. As the car slows to get a closer look, Rabbit whispers, "Just act natural."

Needless to say, the car did not stop. We drove back to town with the lift extended and a deer tied to it. We had to drive in the middle of the road so that the lift wouldn't hit people's mail boxes that were close to the road. It was indeed an adventure.

Rabbit and I have been on many adventures, and through them all I have learned that Ecclesiastes 4: 9, 10, & 12 is true. "Two are better than one, because they have a good return for their work: If one falls down, his friend can help him up. But pity the man who falls and has no one to help him up! Though one may be overpowered, two can defend themselves. A cord of three strands is not quickly broken."

Do you know who the third strand in our unbreakable cord is? I believe it is the Creator of the Universe. I believe it is the King of kings and Lord of lords. Jesus himself has blessed this friendship and blessed our lives.

Well, I gotta go now, friends. One day you'll have to get me to tell you about the time the Rabbit and I got a wheelchair stuck in the woods in the middle of nowhere in the dark and simply had to leave it. We imagined a sheriff's posse investigating the scene and saying, "Don't worry boys, he won't get far on foot."

Tender Moments

Kelly and I were married May 26, 2006. The events surrounding that date are mostly a blur. Any one of them would be enough to stress out most people. On May 18th, just days before the wedding, we closed on our house. Neither of us had ever owned a home, so to say we were a bit nervous would be an understatement.

The next day, the 19th, Kelly graduated with her Master's degree. Big commencement ceremony. Family in town. You know how it goes. The following Tuesday, out of town guests began arriving for the wedding. The rehearsal supper was on Thursday. The wedding was on Friday night. Then, after a brief three night stay in a local resort, we moved into our new home on Monday, Memorial Day. We had to get everything done on Monday, because Tuesday I had to be back at work!

Needless to say, we postponed our "real" honeymoon until the end of the summer. We opted for a six day cruise through Alaska's Inner Passage. It was absolutely beautiful and well worth the wait. At one of our ports-of-call, we were informed we would be "tendering." As you will soon learn, I found this to be quite the misnomer, as there was nothing tender about this ordeal. Tendering, if you don't know, is the process whereby the ship does not dock and allow passengers to walk the gangplank. Instead, you board smaller boats, called tenders, and they shuttle passengers across the bay. I suppose this practice is used when the bay is too shallow to allow the cruise ship to pull close enough to dock. Now, I've never tendered in a little boat across part of the ocean because, well, we don't have an ocean in Conehatta, Mississippi.

Getting on the tender and ferrying across the bay went smoothly. Getting off the tender even worked fine, and Kelly and I enjoyed our excursion in Sitka, Alaska. The return trip is where circumstances began to conspire against us. I believe there were two significant factors that contributed to our troubles. First, the wind and waves had picked up while we were in port. Second, our tender crew must have been the B-team. These guys did not run the well-oiled machine of loading and unloading disabled passengers that our original crew did.

When the tender tied off to the platform on the cruise ship was when things started to concern me. The crew ordered all of the able bodied passengers off first. I think this was a mistake. Picture in your mind a small boat full of passengers. If it has between thirty-five and fifty people in it, it will sit lower in the water and be more stable than without those people. My new bride disembarked, as well. Oh, the love this woman has for me! Inseparable through good times and bad, we are.

After all of the able-bodied passengers had unloaded, the crew decided to try to pull the tender closer for the unloading of the wheelchairs. This proved exceedingly difficult, again because of the higher waves, the lighter vessel, and the incompetence of the crew. Before the tender was close enough to the platform and before it was tied properly, one of the crew tried to connect the wheelchair ramp from the tender to the platform. Does the phrase "fell off in the ocean" mean anything to you?

There was another gentleman in a wheelchair on the tender with me. When he witnessed this event, he turned to me and said, "I'll be glad to let you go first." I'll bet you will! Let me pause here to say there is not a selfish bone in my body. Unfortunately, I was closest to the door. When all was apparently set, one of the crewmen got behind my wheelchair in position to push and said," When I say 'Go!' you go really fast!" You bet I'll go really fast! I'll look like Evel Knievel coming out of this boat.

At this point I looked out on the platform to see my wife, not on her knees praying as a good Baptist wife should have been. No, friends, she had her camera out, aimed to take a picture.

Apparently this was a photo opportunity she could not pass up. Later, when I asked her about this behavior, she said, with a twinkle in her eye, that she intended to capture the moment for fear that she would need conclusive proof of this series of unfortunate events to collect on my life insurance policy.

We all want proof, don't we? We like to have significant evidence supporting our case. Kelly wanted proof that she would be financially secure in the event of my death; however, there is something significantly more important than financial security during a time of death. It is the eternal security of one's soul. Do you know Jesus himself gives us this guarantee? Or, should I say, he *is* our guarantee.

Second Corinthians 1:21-22 says, "Now it is God who makes both us and you stand firm in Christ. He anointed us, set his seal of ownership on us, and put his Spirit in our hearts as a deposit, guaranteeing what is to come." In Christ we have both a seal and a deposit guaranteeing God's ownership of us.

A seal was used in ancient times by kings, usually in the form of a signet ring, to declare things into law. Deposits have been used in more modern times to insure that people will follow through on what they've promised.

I have a lawyer friend who explained to me that, legally, only one is required. Our God gives us both. How great is our God!

Horses I've Known

My Friend "Flicker"

I once heard my father say, "All the rednecks wanna be cowboys." This was not a derogatory statement as he was including himself in that category. Growing up, Dad rode horses, participating in trail rides and other local equestrian events. (My father will laugh when he reads that I called the get-togethers at the Union arena "equestrian events").

As the saying goes, "The apple doesn't fall far from the tree," and I, too, was bitten at an early age by the horse bug. I don't know that "horse" was my *first* word as a child, but it wasn't far behind. In grade school when the teacher asked us to make sentences using our vocabulary words, I would be bent on figuring out a way to squeeze them into sentences about horses or cowboys or something in that genre.

My father and his father co-owned forty acres of land in the New Prospect community near Sebastopol, Mississippi. (Know anyone else from New Prospect, Mississippi? Probably not. The only even semi-famous person I know to have come from there was Turner Catledge, managing editor of the *New York Times* from 1944 to 1970. Just a little trivia. I digress.) To say that I "grew up on a farm" would be a loose interpretation of the phrase, since my father had a full-time job elsewhere, and neither Dad nor Papaw really made any money in this joint-venture. However, there were always thirty or so crossbred cattle on the place, as well as a variety of other livestock, including pigs, chickens, goats, guineas, dogs, cats, and, of course, horses.

Because of my disability, it takes a very special horse to accommodate my needs. To say that I need one that is gentle, slow, and tolerant is quite the understatement. I can vividly remember many Saturdays spent in search of the perfect animal. Papaw assumed the role of Adam on the farm in that he was in charge of naming all the animals, and some of his names were a bit unique.

He also held the superstition that changing an animal's name was bad luck, so we also gained a few animals with interesting names in tow. We had horses named Jubilee, Goldilocks, Sugarfoot, Patsy, Blue, and Gismo. I rode them all, but they all had some personality quirk or bad habit that simply did not fit a boy with cerebral palsy.

That is, until we bought Flicker. She was a beautiful Palomino mare that just seemed to suit my needs perfectly. I can remember asking Papaw what we were going to call her, and he said that she reminded him of Flicker from the TV show. (In my defense, the television series was way before my time. I did not realize until later when corrected, much to my embarrassment, by an

English teacher at school, that the show in fact was entitled, *"My Friend FLICKA"*! Again, I'm from rural Mississippi. We say thangs different down here.)

I also remember that the very afternoon we brought her home, I was given the opportunity to ride independently. Usually, when we were trying out a new horse, Dad would lead me up and down the driveway for many rides until we felt we understood the horse's disposition. Not with Flicker. When Dad saddled her up and told me I could ride in the pasture around where he was cutting firewood, I knew then that she was a very special horse. Shine! Sweet freedom, shine!

I enjoyed many happy hours astride that horse. There were many Saturdays when I would mount up as early in the morning as I could get Dad to tack her, ride until noon when I would go inside to eat a banana and mayonnaise sandwich and watch Mid-South wrestling, and then go back out and ride until dark. Those were the days, and there was nothing else I would have rather been doing.

One beautiful spring day, Dad asked me if I wanted to ride out and check the cows to see if one had given birth to a new calf. Are you kidding me? Would I? I would enjoy nothing more. This is what cowboys do! We go check the cattle. And I am a cowboy! Along with me and Flicker that day was Nailer, Papaw's hound dog. Again, Papaw came up with some unique handles for the animals, and this dog was no different. Whatever images are conjured up in your mind when you hear of a hound dog named Nailer, assume that is exactly what this dog looked like. He was so ugly he was cute. Kinda like E.T.

We rode out from the barn, down through the gully, and up the next hill to survey the situation. As I sat atop Flicker, looking down onto our small herd of cattle, I felt like the Marlboro Man. Little did I know that in the next few minutes I would look more like one of the Three Stooges than an icon of the American West.

I have no idea what possessed that dog to chase those cows, but chase he did; and for a moment I thought he was bringing them to me. I thought that was cool, kind of like a round-up. My joy was short lived, as Flicker decided she wanted to chase the cows, as well. She reared to run, but I clutched the reins tightly and didn't give her the opportunity. The second time she reared, however, my "I-am-a-real-cowboy" big belt buckle collided with the saddle horn, sank deep into my abdomen, and knocked the wind right out of me.

In an instant Flicker bolted. I was no longer upright in the saddle; instead, I was holding on for dear life around the side of her neck. Flicker was a fat horse. Mounting up was a bit like swinging your leg over a fifty-five gallon drum. So, as my weight shifted, the entire saddle began to rotate around to the side of her body so that it, too, was no longer upright.

Now, as if the situation were not bad enough, you need to know that there is a crucial element to this ride that I've neglected to mention. Before I left the barn on my ride that day, my Dad tied me onto the saddle using what is called a "pigin' string." It's what is used by rodeo cowboys to hogtie calves, hence the name. Dad used it to ensure that, if I lost my balance, I would remain in the saddle instead of falling off and breaking something. However, as Flicker's saddle rotated, I realized that this seatbelt of sorts was more of a liability than an asset.

If I had been thrown clear in the midst of her gallop, I might have broken an arm or a collarbone. As it were, if I lost my grip around her neck, I would have wound up underneath the thundering hooves being trampled to death, or my neck would have snapped, killing me instantly. Even as I write this story more than twenty years later, I cringe at how badly this could have ended.

I honestly don't remember if I fell and Flicker stopped instantly, or if when she stopped I was too exhausted to hold on any longer. I believe now that the hand of God grabbed those reins and calmed that animal. I found myself upside down, still tied to the saddle, starring at the undercarriage of this horse. It was a scary moment, yes, but I was thankful to be alive. Luckily, Dad had tied the pigin' string in a slip knot, and with one jerk I set myself free and rolled out from underneath Flicker.

About the time I got to my hands and knees, I saw my Dad walking toward me. He looked like he was crying. He had heard the dog barking and the cattle stampeding and he knew something was terribly wrong. In fact, he expected the worst. It was the first time I'd seen my father cry. That does something to a young man.

I like telling this story for two reasons. First of all, it's a great story. It has humor, adventure, a plot line with a climax, background and characters, and, thankfully, a happy ending. Second, and more importantly, these events brought me to grips with my own mortality, which God used to bring me into a personal relationship with Him through his Son, Jesus Christ.

Lying in bed a few nights later, I realized that if I had been killed during that wild ride, I would have spent eternity in hell separated by my sin from a loving and just God. Hebrews 9:27-28 says, "Just as man is destined to die once, and after that to face judgment, so Christ was sacrificed once to take away the sins of many people; and he will appear a second time, not to bear sin, but to bring salvation to those who are waiting for him."

When you're young, you think you'll live forever.

That ride and this verse taught me different; short of this Second Coming, we will all die. Afterwards we will give an account of how we lived our lives, and we will answer the Father's question, "Why should I let you into my Heaven?" There is only one acceptable answer: "The blood of Jesus has covered my sin."

Those truths scared me to the foot of the Cross. Understand this--before Flicker ran away with me, I knew about God. I even knew about Jesus. I had been to church for nine months before I was even born! I had plenty of religion in my head, but what I needed was a Savior in my heart. The sad truth is that many souls will miss Heaven by just sixteen inches, the distance between their head and their heart. Accepting the precious and perfect gift that Jesus gave us in His death on the cross as the only payment for our sins is the bridge that closes that gap.

Me and Mr. Wilson

My father knows horses. His father before him was a great judge of horseflesh. So it only followed that I would want to become somewhat of a horse-whisperer myself. I can walk on crutches, but Dad and Papaw literally had me on a horse before I could walk. As I got older and stronger and my balance and coordination improved, I was allowed the freedom to ride in the pastures by myself.

On horseback, I found something I'd never known before: independence. I didn't have to bother anyone with pushing me in my manual wheelchair to a particular location. I didn't have to worry whether or not my legs would be able to go a certain distance. I just relied on Jubilee, or Gismo, or Flicka to get me where I was going.

But there's something far more important to a disabled person than independence or freedom. It's called dignity. You see, when I'm on horseback, I can barely be distinguished from an able-bodied rider. These twelve hundred pound four-legged beasts are a great equalizer.

These days I ride horses with a group called Special Equestrians. It's a horseback riding facility for people with physical, mental, and emotional disabilities. I ride on Tuesday mornings for about an hour or so before I have to be at the college to teach my class. I've ridden with them for about four years now, and over that period of time have had several different mounts.

First there was Junior, a beautiful chestnut Quarter horse gelding who reminded me how amazing riding was after so many years out of the saddle. Then there was Cowboy, a muscled, bay-colored Appaloosa gelding, who tested my patience and skills every chance he got.

Now there's Wilson. Whatever you have pictured in your mind that a horse named Wilson would look like, it is exactly right. He's mostly a mutt, long and lanky with maybe some Standard bred Trotter mixed in. His legs look like an eggbeater when he runs, and he has the most awful half-trot/half-pace a rider would ever want to try to sit.

This is the horse that the director, Kathy, and session leader, Ellen, decided I would learn to canter on. For those of you who don't ride, most horses have three gaits: a walk, some form of trot or pace, and then a canter (or what Southerners call a short-lope) that can be urged into a full gallop. My dad always said the horses we owned had three different gaits: start, stumble, and fall. But Papaw said a good horse could "short-lope all day in the shade of a small oak tree."

Cantering is very different than trotting. It is much faster and has a totally different rhythm because it's a three beat gait instead of four like a trot. It's also more dangerous. A large animal moving at speeds ofthirty-five miles per hour is not much deterred by a small piece of metal in its mouth connected to your hands by small leather straps.

I was apprehensive about learning to canter on Junior, but a bad fall that hyper-extended his front leg put him out to pasture before that came to fruition. I was excited about cantering on Cowboy, who had a big and powerful stride, but his bad attitude caused him to be shipped back home. So now there's Wilson. Oh, for pity's sake, Wilson, with his knobby knees and lifeless eyes. Who wants to move to the next level of horsemanship on a Wilson?

So a Tuesday morning in mid-April dawns and it is cold. The radio announcer says the temperature is forty degrees as I get out of my truck at the stables as I described before, my muscles and joints are sometimes uncooperative at best. This gets worse in cold weather. I am warned by Ellen that the horses are "more forward" when it's cold. I'm warned by the lead-walker that Wilson is "feeling a bit frisky" this morning. I know it's going to be a challenge. I felt as if I was going to break in two as I stretched my leg over Wilson's back and settled in to the saddle. The wind began to blow, and it felt like there was nothing between us and the North Pole except a barbed wire fence with two strands down.

But it was time to ride, so ride I did, stiff legs and all. I was feeling insecure, so as I asked Wilson to canter; I put "the death grip" on the saddle horn, holding on to maintain my balance. However, the more I tightened my grip, the stiffer my legs became, and the more I was pushed up out of the saddle. "Bend your knees," Kathy yells, from across the arena. "Easier said than done," I yell back!

Then I heard it, a little voice that said, "Trust Wilson. He's doing all the work. Relax. Let go." So I did. I let go of the saddle horn and gave him his head. And we cantered. No, it wasn't the Kentucky Derby or anything, but we were, as they say, "huntin' some yonder." My legs relaxed, I eased deeper into the saddle, and Wilson and I moved in perfect harmony around the oval.

Isn't that a great picture of our relationship with God? Often times, we're so worried about our insecurities, baggage, and inabilities that we find something in this world to latch onto and we stiffen up; and life never seems to work out like we'd like it too. Isaiah 55:8 says, "For my thoughts are not your thoughts, neither are your ways my ways, declares the LORD." And that voice inside us is the Holy Spirit saying, "Trust God. He's doing all the work. Relax. Let go."

Thank you Mr. Wilson, for reminding me to let go…and let God.

Our Free Will

Imagine my surprise when the session leader at Special Equestrians, the therapeutic horseback riding facility I frequent, explained to our class of disabled riders that since we were more experienced than the other classes, we would now be expected to tack the horses ourselves. For those of you who don't ride, tacking involves grooming the animal and then putting on the blanket, saddle, and bridle.

Tacking a horse is not an easy job for an able bodied rider. The blanket is large and cumbersome, the saddle is heavy, and putting the bridle on involves sticking your fingers in the horse's mouth. I gave it my best effort. My only advantage is that I was tacking Wilson.

Wilson is the biggest "teddy bear" of a horse anyone could wish for. He weighs, literally, half a ton and is as strong as an ox, but he is indeed a gentle giant. This horse will follow my wheelchair around like a puppy dog. He remains perfectly still while I groom him, allowing me to lean my body weight on him for support while I brush his back and mane. Wilson will even stand patiently in an uncomfortable position next to a fence while I go about the slow process of saddling him. Witnessing this, one day the director of the program said, "You know, that horse wouldn't do that for just anybody."

We could all stand to be a little more like Wilson. You see, one of the neatest things about Wilson is that he *allows* his strength to be used. He submits to my control so that I can do what needs to be done. If this animal didn't want to leave his stall, I couldn't make him. If he wanted to jerk away and run while I was leading him, he could. And most of the horses on the face of the earth wouldn't let someone in a wheelchair roll around and push and pull on them like I do with Wilson.

But Wilson and I have a special relationship. It's a relationship built on trust, not unlike the relationship we as Christians have with our Heavenly Father. I lead and Wilson follows. I pull with the right rein, and he turns right. I squeeze with my legs and he moves faster.

This is the picture of a servant's strength. This is the essence of allowing oneself to be positioned in order to receive instruction. This is what it means to be a child of God. In John 14:21, Jesus says, "He who has My commandments and *keeps* them, it is he who loves me. And he who loves Me, will be loved by My Father, and I will love him and manifest Myself to him."

The point is this-- God didn't make us like robots. He gave us the ability to choose whether or not to love or to reject Him. He gave us free will. While on the one hand, this has inherent risks, on the other, it also has unbelievable rewards. Just think for a moment about how incredible it is in your own life when you realize that someone has *chosen* to love you. I'm not talking about a parent or a relative that we feel compelled to love out of obligation, but rather the fondness we feel toward someone who, although once a complete stranger, has now decided to invest himself or herself in our lives.

When I was in college, a friend and mentor of mine, Tim Glaze, posed a question on this subject by asking, "Can God make a rock so heavy that He can't lift it?" It spawns an interesting theological debate. To say "Yes" would somehow call into question God's rock *lifting* ability. However, to say "No" would challenge His rock *making* ability.

Then, in a way that only a good teacher can, my friend delivered the answer with such unmistakable clarity that it made you think about the question even more. Tim said, "Sure He can. He made you and I, didn't He?" With that, the entire conversation was changed from the limitations of the physical to meditation on the spiritual. You see, God can't make us love Him. He can't make us do what's right. That's why it so pleases Him as our Heavenly Father when we come to Him humbly, thankfully, reverently, and say, "Not my will, but *Your* will be done."

Remember when you were little, and you were riding in the car with your Mom? If she had to slam on the breaks, wouldn't she throw her arm in front of you to keep you from banging your head into the dashboard?

God kind of works the same way. He gives us instructions to keep us safe. And when we rebel, it's like we're using our free will to push the arm of God away and say, "No thanks. I can handle this." Don't you dare believe it! I once heard Christian author, Louie Giglio, urge a group of young people, "Stop believing the lie that there's anything out there better than what God has in store for you."

In order for that promise to manifest itself in our lives, we must die to self. We have to come to the place where we realize that our free will is sometimes not our best option. Paul said in Galatians 2:20, "I have been crucified with Christ and I no longer live, but Christ lives in me. The life I live in the body, I live by faith in the Son of God, who loved me and gave himself for me."

Our church family was recently taught Zechariah 8:23 in which a group of people says, "Let us go with you, because we have heard that God is with you." My prayer today is that *your* prayer today would be that others would say that about you; that other people would so see the presence of God in your life, and that they would want to be around you and know what makes you different, joyful, and complete. They will only see that when we surrender our free will to His will and His way.

Third Time's the Charm

I consider myself a well-educated person. I earned a Bachelor's and a Master's degree from a land grant institution that was established in 1878. I consider myself a well-read person. I have conquered the writings of Dostoyevsky and Keats, as well as the Mississippi authors from Faulkner to Grisham. I consider myself a well-spoken person. I have spoken at colleges, camps, and conferences from as close as right here in Birmingham, to as far away as Costa Maya, Mexico, on topics ranging from the economics law of eventually diminishing marginal returns to Biblical topics of hermeneutics and eschatology.

However, I must remind you at this point that I am from the South. I am Southern born and Southern bred, and when I die I'll be Southern dead. Mark Twain said, "I never let my schooling get in the way of my education." I tend to ascribe to that same philosophy, and my "book learning" does not always show through in the analogies I use to illustrate a point.

In my single days, if I found a woman attractive, I might say, "Those rare and golden qualities which you posses have led me to the inescapable conclusion that, to be in your presence thrills my soul," while inside I was probably thinking, "Girl, you're better than a big old blob of mayonnaise dripping out of a spam sandwich." I also use words like "suntnuther" and "widjadidja", just to name a few.

All of these colloquialisms and all of this humor are lost on my new friend, Fransiska. Fransiska is a fifteen year-old foreign exchange student from Germany who volunteers at the stables where I ride horses once a week. I have thought many times how truly difficult it must be to study English from a textbook and then move to the Southeastern United States where very few people speak proper English.

Horses in Germany are still horses, and they really understand neither English nor German. Fransiska's horsemanship was never in question; but her English, well, let's just call it a work in progress. She has enough difficulty with words like "saddle" and "bridle" without me making references to a "Choctaw totin' a hog," or commenting, "Well, I guess we're just gonna have to lick this calf again." Bless her heart.

Given my physical limitations, saddling the tallest pony in the string, Mr. Wilson, is not an easy task. One particular afternoon, Fransiska was holding Wilson's halter to try to keep him steady while I put his blanket on. The saddle blanket is not heavy; it's just big and awkward to manage. As long as I have something to lean on, I can usually maintain my balance while standing up.

At the stables, that "something" is usually a large animal with a mind of its own.

I stood up, and gained my balance; but as I leaned my weight on Wilson, he shifted his body away from the pressure. I lost my balance and had to sit back down in my wheelchair. I stood up a second time, placed the blanket on his back, but not quite high enough, and it slid off. I gathered the blanket and my composure, looked at Fransiska and said "Third time's the charm!" I stood up and laid the blanket perfectly on Wilson's back.

Fransiska stared at me puzzled. "What is *the charm*?" she asked. Ah, a simple question from a humble heart. "The charm is the trick ... the lucky strike...the winner," I said, not really sure I was translating my meaning very clearly. Then she said one of the most profound things I think I have ever heard. "Then why could it not be the *first time?*"

Why indeed, Fransiska! Why is it that things just never seem to work out like you planned, or at least not the first time? Well, I've learned recently that life is a test. The Bible mentions words like trials, temptations, and testing more than 200 times. Nothing is insignificant in your life. Even the smallest incident has significance for your character development. Every day offers an opportunity to deepen your faith, to demonstrate God's love to another human being, or to learn to depend upon God more fully. Some storms will be emotionally or physically devastating, and others you won't even know are happening. Through them you will learn, as Scott Kirpayne sang, "Sometimes He calms the storm, and other times He calms His child."

So once again Mr. Wilson has taught me an important life lesson, and I've decided to pass it on. Here's my challenge: don't get too upset when the first two times don't go exactly as planned. Realize that it is in those times that God is trying to grow us into something more beautiful than we were and trying to mold us into His image.

Let That Pony Run

Dad and I like to watch horse racing. The problem is, we don't know anything about it. We love horses, but as far as knowing anything about breeding or the business of racing, we are pretty delinquent. We just like to, as Dad says, "Watch the ponies run." Growing up, I remember watching the Triple Crown every year, but one year stands out above all the others.

The year was 1989. Every year Dad and I would choose a horse to pull for during the race or races, based on some very shallow indicators like name or color. Very rarely did we know anything of bloodlines, earnings or how they finished in recent races - enough to make educated decisions.

Before the Kentucky Derby, I chose a big Chestnut colored horse named "Easy Goer." This was my pick for a few simple reasons. First, because of his color, he stood out against the usual back drop of all the other bay colored Thoroughbred horses. Secondly, his trainer was named *Shug* McGaughey. It also didn't hurt that the betters had made Easy Goer the favorite to win the Derby.

Dad chose to root for a speedy black colt named "Sunday Silence." This horse may have subconsciously been attractive to Dad because of his fondness for Sunday afternoon siestas.

I don't remember very much about the Kentucky Derby itself, just that Sunday Silence, Dad's horse, won, and my horse, Easy Goer, came in second. The other thing I remember is that I was excited about the rematch in the Preakness a few weeks later. And, man, what a rematch it was! It was the stuff of legends. No Hollywood director, no matter how creative or talented, could have made the clash of these two titans appear any more dramatic.

Sunday Silence broke to the front of the pack early with the pacesetters, while Easy Goer got off to a sluggish start. But when Easy started to make his move, it looked like the other horses were standing still. When he passed the frontrunners, including Sunday Silence, it looked like the race would be a blowout, and he would leave them all in the dust.

Sundays are special, though; and on this particular Saturday, this particular *Sunday* was very special. Sunday Silence's jockey asked for more and his horse responded. As Easy Goer and Sunday Silence started down the home stretch with ¼ mile to go, the 90,000 plus in attendance knew they were witnessing something for the ages.

"Down the stretch they come! Sunday Silence on the outside. Easy Goer on the inside. Stride for stride, neck and neck, nose to nose." And after a photo finish and a stewards review that seemed to last forever…it was Sunday Silence, Dad's horse, who won by a nose.

In my heart I still think Easy won, and three weeks later he did in fact win the Belmont, the last leg of the Triple Crown, by eight lengths; but that's beside the point. (These two had a fourth rendezvous in the Breeders Cup, in which Sunday Silence won by a neck, but that's also beside the point.) The point is this was a moment that will ever be etched in my mind. A moment that Dad and I shared. Ever since then, if I am unable to watch the Triple Crown with my Dad, I call him and we watch it together over the phone. More often than not these days, it seems we're pulling for the *same* horse, for we'd both like to see someone win the Triple Crown.

Though the Bible doesn't talk much about horse racing, Brother Paul does talk about racing in general. Here's one of my favorite passages from Hebrews 12: 1-3, "Therefore, since we are surrounded by such a great cloud of witnesses, let us throw off everything that hinders and the sin that so easily entangles, and let us run with perseverance the race marked out for us. Let us fix our eyes on Jesus, the author and perfecter of our faith, who for the joy set before him endured the cross, scorning its shame, and sat down at the right hand of the throne of God. Consider him who endured such opposition from sinful men, so that you will not grow weary and lose heart."

A couple things to consider from these verses. First, the part about "throwing off everything that hinders" reminds me of another horse race. It's the one at the end of "The Black Stallion" movie. You know, the one about the little boy and the big horse. In the big race, they've dressed the boy up in a bunch of garb so that the spectators won't realize he's just a kid. Midway through, he just throws off his helmet and goggles he's been told to wear so that he can ride the Black as they've done so many times before. God help us to cast off those things that hinder our relationship with Him and keep us from running the race set before us.

Second, let's talk about this "fixing our eyes on Jesus" part. Did you know that many race horses wear blinders on their bridle that allow them to only look forward? That way they are not distracted by the crowd or other horses or anything else. They just run!

Turn your eyes upon Jesus.
Look full in His wonderful face,
And the things of earth will grow strangely
*   dim*
In the light of His glory and grace.

Keeps everything in perspective, doesn't it?

Random Thoughts

The Painted House

The sign reads, "Paint House. Not like fence. No up, down. Paint house side to side. (1/2 right hand, 1/2 left hand.)" Remember the movie? Of course you do. All of us "children of the '80's" remember "The Karate Kid." I caught part of this movie the other night and realized something I'd never thought about before. Tucked away in the middle of this motion picture is a great Biblical truth.

Now, for those of you who may have forgotten, after Mr. Miyagi rescues Daniel from the Cobras, he promises to teach him karate if Daniel promises to do exactly as he instructs with no questions. Well, Daniel spends the next several days waxing cars, painting fences, and sanding floors. After spending all day painting the guy's house while he's off fishing, Daniel is pretty ticked. "Did you ever think I might have wanted to go fishing, too?" Daniel asks. "You not here when I leave," Mr. Miyagi says. Daniel says, "I thought I was gonna learn karate." "You learn plenty," says Mr. Miyagi. Daniel has had enough waxing, painting and sanding and announces, "I'm going home!"

This is the turning point of the movie, where the rubber meets the road. Mr. Miyagi says, "Daniel-son show me wax on, wax off." Over the next couple of minutes those boring or repetitive "household chore"- type arm motions are transformed into karate blocks by the Master. At the end of this brief training session, Mr. Miyagi throws a flurry of punches and kicks, and Daniel blocks every one! He walks away amazed at his accomplishments.

In the book of James, Chapter 1, verses 2 through 6, it is written: "Consider it pure joy, my brothers, whenever you face trials of many kinds, because you know that the testing of your faith develops perseverance. Perseverance must finish its work so that you may be mature and complete, not lacking anything. If any of you lacks wisdom, he should ask God, who gives generously to all without finding fault, and it will be given to him. But when he asks, he must believe and not doubt, because he who doubts is like a wave of the sea, blown and tossed by the wind."

So many times we ask God, "Why"? Why am I going through all this? Well, here's our answer. We're in training! God is preparing us for the trials that are going to come later. As the verses say, these trials are developing our perseverance (or patience) so that we can be mature and complete. The verses also say that God is not stingy with his wisdom and will give it generously to those who ask believing.

There's another reason we get to go through troubles. 2 Corinthians 1:4 says, "He comforts us in all our troubles, so that we can comfort those in any trouble with the comfort we ourselves have received from God." It's all about perspective. It's all about realizing that life is about way more than what you're going through right then and there. Even those repetitive "household chore"-type things, like Bible study, prayer time, Sunday school, and tithing are only a small part of a bigger picture.

So thank you, Daniel LaRusso. Thank you, Mr. Miyagi. Thank you for teaching us that "wax on, wax off" is less about buffing cars to a shine and more about polishing us into the gems God wants us to be.

The Recession, New Years and Newman Road

I'm an Economics instructor by trade. The current recession is what we in academia call a "teachable moment." We've had several discussions in my classes about how best to stimulate the economy. There are basically two opposing viewpoints.

There are some who believe the "Government Expenditure Multiplier Theory" that asserts that for every dollar increase in government spending there will be an even greater increase in Gross Domestic Product (GDP). Proponents of this theory, called Keynesians, claim that if the government decides to build a road, for example, that a new job has been created for the person working on the road. That person now has income that they would not have had otherwise, they will now spend money, and the economy will be stimulated.

The opposing viewpoint comes from the "Consumer Sovereignty" or "Classical" Economists. Their theory is that in a free marketplace, consumers are in control and the more money they have in their hands to spend, the better. They reject the "government should spend more" theory, pointing out that, unless you believe in the Tooth Fairy, the money that the government spends must be taken from consumers, through taxes. Those consumers could have stimulated the economy more had they had more money in their pockets with which to stimulate it.

Keynesians would argue, however, that cutting taxes does not stimulate the economy. Polling data that indicates when people are asked, "If you received a tax cut or refund check, what would you do with the money?" The majority of respondents say they would use the money to pay off debt, or they would put it into savings. Keynesians are quick to point out that neither of these would stimulate the economy. Classically, however, consumers spend what they get, and those promises to pay off debt or put the money into savings are almost as reliable as New Year's resolutions.

Speaking of the New Year, I'm not much on resolutions, but I did resolve once to begin a scripture memory course. The first scripture suggested for memorizing was 2 Corinthians 5:17, "Therefore, if any man be in Christ, he is a *new creature*: old things are passed away; behold, all things are become *new*" (*emphasis added*). That's a great verse, and very timely as we begin 2011. Many months after that, I received a letter from a summer missionary who was living at "4000 Newman Road." Do you see it? *New-Man* Road!

I thought it too much to be just a coincidence. Think about it! "If any man is in Christ, he is a new creature…a new creation…a new *man*!" As followers of Christ, we should all be traveling this "new man road," shouldn't we? This process of denying ourselves, taking up our cross, and following Jesus is a daily task.

Another verse that relates to "Newman Road" and becoming a "new creation" is 1 Corinthians 13:11 which says, "When I was a child, I spoke as a child, I understood as a child, I thought as a child: but *when I became a man*, I put away childish things" (*emphasis added*).

I must admit, this verse made me a little miffed at Brother Paul. Here he tells us what he was like before he became a man and what he is like now that he has become a man, but he never tells us *when* he became a man. He doesn't tell us where he was, or what he was doing, or if there was some type of ceremony. Now, this is purely speculation on my part, but I don't think Paul was talking about his Bar mitzvah. I think it happened when he was traveling down a road. The Damascus Road. A road not unlike this "Newman Road."

May I humbly suggest something to you? Make a resolution to read the Book of Acts. Pay particular attention to the ninth chapter. I think you'll agree that our road and Paul's road start at the same place, and that both roads set us on the path to becoming new creatures. The road to real "newness" begins at the point where we realize that we're not in charge, and we meet the One who is. To quote Robert Frost, *"Two roads diverged in a wood, and I-- I took the one less traveled by, and that has made all the difference."*

Summer Time…..Blues?

In his book "The Four Pillars of a Man's Heart", Stu Weber writes about Camelot. Remember Camelot? King Authur. The Knights of the Roundtable. Pristine. Pure rivers. Gentle breezes. Children at play. The poets called it "The kingdom of summer." The cast of the 1960 Broadway musical "Camelot" would sing the title song by Alan Jay Lerner and announce:

In short there's simply not,
A more congenial spot,
For happy-ever-aftering
Than here……in Camelot.

Remember when summer was special? Remember when the days lasted forever? Remember homemade ice-cream, and county fairs, and fishing with Dad and, well……summer. Do you know what made Camelot special? The king was on his throne, and the knights were men of honor. They were men of courage, conviction, compassion, and, believe it or not, love.

1 Corinthians 13 is known as the "Love Chapter", the greatest dissertation ever written on the subject. In this chapter the Apostle Paul, the greatest knight of the faith ever, tells us something about love. Now for most guys this isn't really our

strong suit. But I think maybe Paul was trying to tell us "Fellas, if you wanna be *real* men, real knights in God's kingdom, then you better learn how to love, and you better get it right!"

And he's not talking about a Hollywood romanticized version of love. He's talking about *real* love... loved by *real* men. This is the kind of love that takes action. Listen to what he writes in the seventh verse of this chapter:"(Love) always protects, always trusts, always hopes, always perseveres." This is especially true of the love for the bride of Christ, "the body" that he talks about in Chapter 12.

See, in Chapter twelve Paul goes on and on about how important it is to have unity in diversity, and how important all these spiritual gifts are. But then, in Chapter 13 verses 1-3 and 8-9, he says all of that means *nothing* ... without love. When you realize how much of his heart and soul Paul has poured into chapter twelve, then you can realize how meaningless everything is without love and how true love brings everything into perspective.

As Paul closes out his first letter to the church at Corinth, he challenges us in chapter 16, verse 13 to be, as the Knights of the Roundtable were, men of conviction, and courage, and compassion. Our parent's generation will tell you that, on the whole, our generation is lacking all three. They say that any wind will blow us, that we won't take a stand for anything, and we only care about ourselves. I take that as a personal challenge. I would to God that we would attempt to prove them wrong. Oh, and one more thing, in verse 14, Paul reminds us once again...to love!

"The kingdom of summer," huh? What if we showed everyone that the King of Kings is on the throne of our hearts and that we are men of honor? Then maybe the same thing would be said of us as was said of the apostles in Acts 17:6, "These that have turned the world upside down are come hither also."

Knowing God

Did you ever see or hear the famous comedy duo Abott and Costello do their "Who's on First?" routine? If not, go look it up on the internet. It's hilarious. Comedians would call this humor "circularity," because each question brings an "answer" that leads not to knowledge, but to more puzzling questions. Now take a look at this passage from the Gospel of John and see if you see any similarities. In chapter 14:2-10 Jesus is speaking:

²In my Father's house are many rooms; if it were not so, I would have told you. I am going there to prepare a place for you.

(I've always thought this was an unusual phrase for Jesus to use. "If it were not so, I would have told you that it were not so." Why not just say, "I'm telling you the truth! Daddy's got lots of room!")

³And if I go and prepare a place for you, I will come back and take you to be with me that you also may be where I am.

(Can't you just hear the disciples thinking, "But aren't we ALREADY where you are?)

⁴You know the way to the place where I am going."

⁵Thomas said to him, "Lord, we don't know where you are going, so how can we know the way?"

⁶Jesus answered, "I am the way and the truth and the life. No one comes to the Father except through me.

(Just tell me who's on first, for goodness sake!
Just show me "the way" for goodness sake!)

⁷If you really knew me, you would know my Father as well. From now on, you do know him and have seen him."

⁸Philip said, "Lord, show us the Father and that will be enough for us."

(Who's on first? What's on second? I don't know's on third. "I haven't seen a thing, and I still don't know the way, or where in the wide-wide world of sports you're going!")

⁹Jesus answered: "Don't you know me, Philip, even after I have been among you such a long time? Anyone who has seen me has seen the Father. How can you say, 'Show us the Father'?

¹⁰Don't you believe that I am in the Father, and that the Father is in me? The words I say to you are not just my own. Rather, it is the Father, living in me, who is doing his work.

(By now Philip's got to be about to blow a gasket! "You are in who, and who is in you?")

I will pause here to say that I think at this point, Jesus would just shake his head, and grin, or maybe even chuckle. Now, I know that that thought may go against popular opinion. We have been taught to think that Jesus was always somber, and you may think it sacrilege to compare the Lord and Creator of the universe to Abbott and Costello. But is it so far fetched to think that Jesus had a sense of humor? I mean, he did, after all, invent it!

Now we've thought about "Who's on first," but the real issue here is "Who do we want to know?" That is the question that longs to be answered in verses seven and nine when Jesus says, "If you knew me" and "Don't you know me?" So that's the question I ask myself, and I ask you today. Do you know Him? I'm not asking if you know *of* Him or *about* Him, but do you know Him?

Now that begs the next question: "How do we get to know God?" Well, here are a few verses to help us get started. 2 Chronicles 7:14-15 says, "If my people, who are called by my name, will humble themselves and pray and seek my face and turn from their wicked ways, then will I hear from heaven and will forgive their sin and will heal their land. Now my eyes will be open and my ears attentive to the prayers offered in this place." I think that's our first step. To seek His face. To be no longer content with following blindly in His footsteps but to desire to know Him better and more intimately. To see Him face to face!

There is, however, a warning that comes with this quest. In Exodus 33: 18, 20-23 it is written, "Then Moses said, 'Now show me your glory.' (But the Lord) said, 'You *cannot see my face*, for no one may see me and live.' Then the LORD said, 'There is a place near me where you may stand on a rock. When my glory passes by, I will put you in a cleft in the rock and cover you with my hand until I have passed by. Then I will remove my hand and you will see my back; but *my face must not be seen*'" (*emphasis added*).

Now, why is it that God would in one verse tell us to seek His face, and in another tell us that if we see it we will die? I think the answer is found in these two verses: "I have been crucified with Christ and I no longer live, but Christ lives in me. The life I live in the body, I live by faith in the Son of God, who loved me and gave himself for me" (Galatians 2:20). "For you died, and your life is now hidden with Christ in God" (Ephesians 3:3).

Christ came that we might see God, that we might see His face. But in order to do that we must die to ourselves and be hidden in Christ, just like God hid Moses in the cleft of the rock. Check out Hebrews 1:3, "The Son is the radiance of God's glory and the *exact* representation of his being, sustaining all things by his powerful word. After he had provided purification for sins, he sat down at the right hand of the Majesty in heaven" (*emphasis added*).

My prayer for you is that the honest cry of your heart to the Lord would be, "I want to know you more!"

You Get What You Pay For

As is true for any married couple where both parties work, it is rare for Kelly and me to spend a weekday afternoon home alone together. However, since we both work in education, our schedules do coincide occasionally, and there are those rare instances between semesters that we are less like ships passing in the night. (To say that we both work in education needs more clarification. Kelly teaches three year-old preschool, and I teach economics at a community college. I jokingly say that Kelly gets students before they go to school, and I get them after they finish school, and there is not much change in between.)

One August afternoon we were just hanging out at the house. I was chatting on the phone with my Dad and getting ready to watch the Braves game. There was a knock at the door, and Kelly answered it while I wrapped up my phone conversation. When I was finished, Kelly informed me that the young lady at the door had said that she was working for a carpet cleaning service that was planning to open a new location in our area.

They were in our neighborhood offering to clean a room in your home for free, in the hope that when the store was open, you might recommend their services to friends and family. I thought to myself, "Free! Man, yeah! Let me find you a room. Let's get the biggest room. I'll help move the furniture around if need be." (Isn't that just like human nature to want something for nothing?)

Unbeknownst to me, Kelly was planning a surprise birthday party for me in a few days, and the carpet could have used a good cleaning. We lived in a brand new sub-division, and red mud seemed to always find its way inside via hitching a ride on my wheelchair tires.

The first thing the lady did was ask to borrow our vacuum cleaner. Kelly and I thought this was an odd request, but she decided to play along, and I went to the study to check e-mail. When I can back into the living room, you can imagine my surprise to find a very large man (6'3", 250 lbs.) giving my wife the full-scale sales job on the Name Brand* Vacuum Cleaner. Allow me to pause here to say we were duped! The young lady at the door had simply lied. Had we known that a free carpet cleaning would cost us the next three hours of our lives, we would have promptly declined.

The pitch goes something like this. They use your vacuum first, followed by the Name Brand to prove to you how much filth your vacuum is missing. After the young lady had vacuumed our living room with our vacuum cleaner, then this mountain of a man (we'll call him John for the sake of conversation) proceeded to show us what the Name Brand could accomplish.

During his demonstration, John would vacuum for a minute or two, and then stop the machine to show Kelly and me how dirty the filter was. He repeated this process over, and over, and over again. By the time he was finished there must have been twenty-five or thirty filters spread all over our living room floor! It makes for a startling visual aid.

The idea is to show the potential customer that the current vacuum they own is simply not getting the job done. At this point John looks at me and asks how much I would pay for a high quality vacuum cleaner such as this. I told him I was prepared to write him a check for $50 *immediately*!

John then proceeds to start shampooing our carpet. Again, I must confess that the Name Brand works wonders. That red mud that had been ground in just seemed to come right up with the greatest of ease. The neatest thing is that the shampooing process used a dry foam that did not leave the carpet wet. You could walk on it as soon as you were finished. I must say I was impressed. John then asked something like, "*Now* how much would you pay for it?" I said, "Man, I'll give you $100 *cash* for it!"

Soon after, John's supervisor comes in. We'll call him Stan.* He asks if John was doing a good job and if the carpet was clean. Then we entered into a conversation that, quite honestly, I was not prepared for.

Stan: How much do you think you and your wife could *afford* to pay *per month* for this amazing machine?

Justin: Man, I'm on the Dave Ramsey plan. I don't do anything *per month*! How much is the vacuum cleaner?

Stan: $1,800

Justin: For a *vacuum cleaner*!? Thank you, but no thank you.

Stan: Well, I know my boss will kill me, but I could probably let you have it for $900.

Justin: Sir, that well may be a great deal, but I'm not prepared to spend $900 for a vacuum cleaner, when I could get one at Wal-Mart for $75.

Stan: You see how well that one from Wal-Mart is cleaning your carpet now, right? And you know that if this is not kept clean, in just a few years your wife is going to want new carpet. Then how much is it going to cost you?

Justin: You don't know my wife! In a few years, she's going to want new carpet in this house *no matter* how clean this is!

Stan: Well, I don't usually mention things like this, but you said a few minutes ago that John did a good job on your carpet.

Justin: Oh, yes sir. He did an excellent job.

Stan: Did he tell you that he is one of the front runners for a contest for the top sales representative, and that if he wins, he and his wife will win a trip to Jamaica? John, how many more do you think you'd have to sell to win that trip?

John: I think *one* more would do it.

Justin: I'll give you $200 for the Name Brand.

And with that, Stan and John packed up their Name Brand, walked out of our living room, and walked out of our lives forever.

In retrospect, we were lied to and duped into listening to a sales pitch, but the truth is we *invited* them into our home. Sin often works the same way. Yes, the Deceiver will sometimes come as an angel of light to tempt us. But often times, we Christians simply know better.

To quote John Piper in his book <u>A Godward Life</u>, "If you consistently reject God's counsel in one area, can you really say that your heart is an obedient heart, even if you outwardly comply with other commandments? We delight in the prospect of ongoing assurance and hope, which is jeopardized and weakened if we gradually slip away from Him in callous disobedience" (p.227).

I once heard someone say, "Sin will take you further away than you ever intended. It will make you stay longer than you ever imagined. And it will make you pay a price higher than you ever dreamed existed." Sin is what separates us from a holy God. And Romans 6:23a says, "The wages of sin is death," and that death is an eternal separation from God. That, dear friend, is a high price to pay for temporary pleasure. Much higher than the price of any vacuum cleaner.

* Names were changed to protect the "innocent".

A Great
Game,
But A
Lousy God

Watching T.V.'s Not All Bad

For the better part of eight years, my job was evening coordinator for a college. I worked 2-10 pm Monday through Thursday, then "regular office hours" on Fridays. That was my schedule for all except about eight weeks of the year, when the college was between semesters and there were no night classes. During those times I worked day shift, and at night I caught up on my TV watching. For a long time I thought I might be missing stuff on TV 'cause I was working at night. WRONG! However, I did see a few neat things, so I put on my "God goggles" and wrote down a few things I learned.

First, on May 18th 2004, I watched Randy Johnson, of the Arizona Diamondbacks, at the age of 40, pitch a perfect game against the Atlanta Braves. For those who don't know baseball, let me try to explain what that means. I'm not talking just about a "no-hitter", although he did strike out 13 of the 27 batters he faced. It was a *perfect* game. He didn't walk anyone, he didn't hit anyone with a pitch, and he committed no errors. *THERE WERE NO BASE RUNNERS FOR THE OPPOSING TEAM.* Up until that point, it had only been done 17 times in Major League history.

Did you know there are *two* ways to get to heaven? 1) Accept Jesus Christ as your Lord and

Savior, or 2) Live a *perfect* life. Do you know how many times the second way has been done in Major League history? In all of history? Only once. Jesus himself is the only person to have lived a sinless life and satisfied God's requirement for righteousness. Romans 6:18-19 says, "Consequently, just as the result of one trespass was condemnation for all men, so also *the result of one act of righteousness was justification* that brings life for all men. For just as through the disobedience of the one man the many were made sinners, so also *through the obedience of the one man the many will be made righteous*"(*emphasis added*).

During my rare night time viewing, I also watched wrestling. My buddies in college used to say, "There are two kinds of men in the world, those who watch wrestling... and those who lie and say they don't!" This statement may or may not be true. I am convinced of one thing, however. I believe there are people watching wrestling and at the same time people are watching religious programming, and both are asking the same question--"Is it real?"

My question to you is the same. Is it real? 2 Timothy 4:2 says, "Preach the word! *Be ready* in season and out of season. Convince, rebuke, exhort, with all longsuffering and teaching."

1 Peter 3:15 says, "But in your hearts set apart Christ as Lord. *Always be prepared* to give an answer to everyone who asks you to give the reason for the hope that you have. But do this with gentleness and respect" (*emphasis added*).

It was also during this time that I watched a "made for TV movie" called "Reversible Errors." It's a courtroom/murder mystery drama. Here are a few quotes and the scripture they reminded me of:

- The movie says, "Beware of building castles on half-acre lots."
  BUT Jesus says in Matthew 7:24-27, "Therefore everyone who hears these words of mine and puts them into practice is like a wise man who built his house on the rock. The rain came down, the streams rose, and the winds blew and beat against that house; yet it did not fall, because it had its foundation on the rock. But everyone who hears these words of mine and does not put them into practice is like a foolish man who built his house on sand. The rain came down, the streams rose, and the winds blew and beat against that house, and it fell with a great crash."
- The movie says, "The plain and simple truth is rarely plain, and never simple."

BUT Jesus says in John 14:6, "I am the way and the truth and the life. No one comes to the Father except through me."

- The movie says, "Better is cold pizza in a quiet place with the woman you love than the best meal in the fanciest restaurant in town."
BUT Proverbs 15:17 says, "Better a meal of vegetables where there is love than a fattened calf with hatred."

I enjoyed the guilty pleasures of evening television but realized there was nothing I needed in it. What do you need most today? Do you need just a word of hope? That's what we all need. And that's what the Word of God does that nothing and no one else can. The Word of God says to us that there is no hopeless situation, no hopeless circumstance, and no hopeless environment. If there were such things, then God would have given up long ago.

Our Team Will Win!

As I write this, my wife and I have approximately thirteen days left until the birth of our first child, and it is thirty days away from the 2008 college football season. My wife might argue that she doesn't know which one I am more excited about. The truth is, I am certainly more excited about the birth of my son, and the kickoff of College Football '08 is a *distant* second ....but it is certainly second! It is now late July, and where we live that means the weather is hot and humid morning, noon, and night. A couple weeks ago, however, we went out to eat supper, and as we came out of the restaurant a cool breeze blew across the parking lot. "Feels almost like fall," Kelly said, to which I replied, "Feels almost like football!"

I graduated from Mississippi State University, and I am a huge Bulldog football fan. Anyone who knows anything about Southeastern Conference football will now be extremely puzzled. How could anyone who is an MSU fan get this excited about football season? For those of you who are not rabid college football fans, allow me to explain.

Mississippi State University's football program has a long and glorious history of losing.

The basketball program has won four SEC

Western Division titles in the last six seasons, posted seven twenty win campaigns in the past decade, and appeared in five NCAA Tournaments in the last seven years. The Diamond Dogs, State's baseball program, was for many years the gold standard in the conference, and longtime coach Ron Polk guided six squads to the College World Series and twenty teams to NCAA regional showings. But woe unto the Bulldog fan when it comes football season.

MSU's football team, however, is a perennial cellar dweller. Between 2000 and 2006 we had exactly zero winning seasons. During that time we had humiliating losses to recently upgraded from D-1 AA Troy State during our homecoming, D-1 AA Maine (most people in the South don't even think Maine has a football team), and double digit losses to UAB and Vanderbilt. In a word, we are *BAD*. It is a miracle if our team can even huddle up and call a play, much less run one.

I must digress and talk about something much more important than football. Do you want to know who ultimately wins? Christians. The winners are those who have placed their trust in the saving power of Jesus Christ. Read the book of Revelations. I know it's crazy. It's got beasts with multiple heads, and plagues, and end-of-the-world kind of stuff. There is, however, joy to be found in knowing how the game ends. Here are a few excerpts from Chapter 19 versus 11, 14, 15, 19 and 20, and Chapter 21:3-4.

"I saw heaven standing open and there before me was a white horse, whose rider is called Faithful and True. With justice he judges and makes war. The armies of heaven were following him, riding on white horses and dressed in fine linen, white and clean. Out of his mouth comes a sharp sword with which to strike down the nations. He will rule them with an iron scepter. He treads the winepress of the fury of the wrath of God Almighty.

Then I saw the beast and the kings of the earth and their armies gathered together to make war against the rider on the horse and his army. But the beast was captured, and with him the false prophet who had performed the miraculous signs on his behalf. With these signs he had deluded those who had received the mark of the beast and worshiped his image. The two of them were thrown alive into the fiery lake of burning sulfur.

And I heard a loud voice from the throne saying, 'Now the dwelling of God is with men, and he will live with them. They will be his people, and God himself will be with them and be their God. He will wipe every tear from their eyes. There will be no more death or mourning or crying or pain, for the old order of things has passed away."

Are you tired of being bullied? Are you tired of being defeated? Are there days it seems like the world and all that is in it is against you? May you rest in this thought, dear brother. Take comfort in these words, dear sister. There will one day be a reckoning. There will one day be victory. There will one day be peace.

In the end, the real "good guy" wins, and the Evil Empire doesn't.

I'm With Him

On October 13, 2001, my alma mater, Mississippi State University, suffered quite possibly their most humiliating football defeat of the modern era. The Bulldogs lost to the Troy State University Trojans (since then renamed the University of Troy) by a score of 9-21.

As a Bulldog fan, this was depressing for a couple different reasons. First, MSU in the preceding four seasons had more success on the gridiron than in the previous 40 years combined. In 1998 Mississippi State won the SEC's Western Division title and a trip to play in the championship game in Atlanta versus eventual national champion, the University of Tennessee. The season after that MSU returned to Atlanta, but this time capping off a 10-2 year with a Peach Bowl victory over Clemson. In 2000, State fought its way to an 8-4 record with its final win of the season coming in what Dog fans refer to as the "Snow Bowl," a memorable 43-41 over-time victory against Texas A&M in the Shreveport, Louisiana, Independence Bowl. These were exciting times in Bulldog football. After that, things truly went downhill.

The second reason the Troy loss was such an embarrassment to the MSU faithful is that the Trojans were literally not even in the same league!

Mississippi State University plays Division 1-A college football. It is the league that most casual observers think of when they think of collegiate athletics. At the time Troy was in Division 1-AA. It is a sub-division. Nevertheless, they were a scrappy bunch, taking on all comers, willing to go anywhere and play anyone in order to earn their stripes and run with the big dogs. On this particular Saturday afternoon, they not only ran with the big dogs, they beat them soundly.

I remember very little about the game itself. What I do remember are the events surrounding it. I took with me to the game that day my nephew Alex, who was about nine at the time. It became a tradition during these years for us to venture at least once a year to Starkville, Mississippi to watch our beloved Bulldogs play ball. The other thing I remember about that afternoon: it rained a flood!

I know that God promised us he would never again destroy the earth with water, and I am not one to doubt the promises of the Almighty, but on that day, my middle name was "Thomas." It was absolutely awful. I thought we'd need a boat to get back to the parking lot. The storm blew so fiercely at one point that the game was halted by the officials, both teams were sent to locker rooms, and Davis-Wade Stadium at Scott Field was ordered cleared. Many of the 20,000 some odd fans in attendance simply left and went home, but many of us sought shelter under the concrete bleachers, and weathered the storm in relative comfort.

At one point during all this, as the torrential rain fell, and the wind blew, and the lighting flashed, and the thunder rolled and the warning sirens rang, and the people scrambled for cover, I realized that this scene might be intimidating for a nine year-old. So I asked Alex, "Are you scared?" "No," was his only reply. "Why not?," I asked for clarification. "Because," he replied, "I'm with you. You always keep me safe, and you know how to get me home."

Have you trusted Jesus to that extent? In Matthew 18:3, Jesus said: "I tell you the truth, unless you change and become like little children, you will never enter the kingdom of heaven." I believe that the change of which Jesus was speaking was a change of heart. More specifically, I think He was saying that we have to give up trying to figure out a way to get to Heaven on our own merit or accomplishment and completely trust in Him.

May I encourage you today? Trust God's promises. He promises us His *presence* in Matthew 28:20b when Jesus says, "Surely I am with you always, to the very end of the age." He promises us a *place* in Heaven. Jesus is quoted in John 14:1-3: "Do not let your hearts be troubled. Trust in God; trust also in me. In my Father's house are many rooms; if it were not so, I would have told you. I am going there to prepare a place for you. And if I go and prepare a place for you, I will come back and take you to be with me that you also may be where I am." Finally, He promises *peace* in Philippians 4:7 which reads, "And the peace of God, which transcends all understanding, will guard your hearts and your minds in Christ Jesus."

A simple prayer from a humble heart: I'm with you. You always keep me safe, and you know how to get me home.

Meditations on Romans 8:28

Introduction

I once heard the story told that when Abraham Lincoln was president, he sent his advisors in search of a phrase or sentence that would be perfect for any occasion. Lincoln wanted to be able to use the same phrase to uplift and inspire the country during her most trying hours, but also to keep us humble and focused during our greatest triumphs. The phrase that was returned was, "This too shall pass."

I recently did an internet search on the phrase. Very quickly I understood that the origins of the phrase are somewhat of a mystery. One of the first things I found was this quote by Lincoln. "It is said an *eastern monarch* once charged his wise men to invent a sentence, to be ever in view, and which should be true and appropriate in all times and situations. They presented him with the words, 'And this, too, shall pass away.' How much it expresses! How chastening in the hour of pride! How consoling it is in the depths of affliction!" Evidently the phrase was not a Lincoln original. The quotation is in *The Way of the Sufi* by Idries Shah, and is the title of a poem by Lanta Wilson Smith. I even read an article (on a site which encouraged readers to quit smoking, of all things!), that the "eastern monarch" that Lincoln referred to was none other than King Solomon. The story there is that Solomon sent *his* advisors in search of a ring that he had seen in a dream, and that one of them met an old jeweler who carved the inscription into a simple gold band. Despite his massive wealth, the great King never seemed to be content, and the phrase on the ring brought him peace.

We have no record of this story in the Bible. 2 Peter 3:10 does mention that when the Lord returns, "The heavens will disappear with a roar; the elements will be destroyed by fire, and the earth and everything in it *shall pass away*" (*emphasis added*). But that's not quite the same. A much more similar phrase would be found in Ecclesiastes 3:1 which says, "There is a time for everything, and a season for every activity under heaven."

But I digress. All of this is really beside the point. There is a verse in the Bible that makes "This too shall pass" pale in comparison. It is verse often misquoted by Christians and non-Christians alike. It is Romans 8:28.

> *And we know*
> *that in all things*
> *God works for the good*
> *of those who love him,*
> *who have been called*
> *according to his purpose.*

And We Know

Romans 8:28 begins with the phrase "And we know". Not "we think," or "we imagine," or "we choose to believe," or "we formed a committee and voted," It says we *know*! But how do we "know" something? There is a worldview that says there is no way of truly knowing anything, that truth is relative and memories are all figments of the imagination. Allow me to begin by explaining what "knowing" is not.

I have a friend named Houston Everett. When we first met, Houston was probably ten or twelve, and I was in my late twenties. Houston and I have a few things in common. We are both from the great state of Mississippi. We both love Mississippi State University. And we both have cerebral palsy. CP affects different people in different ways. Houston's hands and legs and mine are probably equally affected, but the condition has also affected Houston's speech. Every sentence is a laborious effort.

This, however, does not prevent us from yelling at the umpires during MSU baseball games. Houston and I are creative in our heckling. We say things like, "Hey, Blue! If you had one good eye, you'd be a Cyclops!" Or, "Hey, Ump! If you're gonna cheat, you gotta cheat both ways! You're missing a great game out here!" Maybe we'd say something like, "Hey, Blue! Your wife called. She left a message. She said your glasses are still on the night stand!"

But maybe my all time favorite was when Houston, this twelve year-old kid, confined to a wheelchair because of cerebral palsy, with his speech impaired, yelled out, "Hey, Blue! Don't make me come down there and take matters into my own hands!" I responded the only way I knew how. I also yelled at the umpire, "That's right Ump! It would be embarrassing to get beat up by two crippled guys in front of all these people!"

Later, I asked Houston what had made him so upset. He said that the umpire had blown the call, indicating a ball when it was clearly a strike. Playing devil's advocate, I explained to Houston that clearly the official, who was literally right on top of the action, was obviously in a much better position to view such things than we were at thirty yards away. "How do you *know* it was the wrong call," I asked. Houston replied, "Because he called it against *us*!"

This is *not* an example of truly knowing. This is an example of seeing the world in the way that we want it to be. In this case, Houston was viewing things through maroon colored glasses. And I must admit that, on occasion, we all have a tendency to do this. However, this is not the case with the author of our text verse, the Apostle Paul.

When Paul writes "And we know," he is speaking of much more than head knowledge.

This word "know" has several possible translations. I am no Bible scholar, but here's what I've gathered. The word "know" used here could come from the same root as the Greek word "eidon," which means "to see." My understanding is that to have seen or perceived is equivalent to knowing or having knowledge of. It is a perfect tense verb with a present meaning. I find that translation very interesting considering the rest of the verse. Paul here could be saying that "we have *seen* that all things really do work together for good...," but I might be getting ahead of myself. The word "know" is also a Jewish idiom for sexual intercourse between a man and a woman. That would indicate a very intense and intimate knowledge.

My favorite translation, however, is that "to know" means "to have experienced." I think this is the best kind of knowing. Here's why: I could write page after page about what it is like to have cerebral palsy. I could explain how difficult it is to get dressed in the morning or to pick up a pen that has fallen underneath a desk or a hundred other things that most people take for granted everyday. I could be clear, concise, and articulate with my descriptions. I could make you feel guilty and possibly help you appreciate all of the many little blessings in your life.   And, maybe, after all of that, you might say "Now I *know* what it's like to have cerebral palsy."   But you would not *know*. You would not know because you would not have experienced it.   You would not have lived it as Houston and I have.

So Paul is saying, "We have *experienced* God working in all things for the good of those who love him, who have been called according to his purpose."   And that, my friends, is a knowing like no other.

That In All things

Monty Roberts, real life horse whisperer and hero of mine, says in one of his books, "There is no such thing as teaching, only learning." Having said that, when I am asked what I do for a living, I say that I try to teach economics at Jefferson State Community College. I think the word "try" is important here, because if students are not learning, then I am only talking and not teaching.

Jeff State has a student enrollment of about 7,000, with an increasing number of international students. I've often thought how difficult it must be to learn English from a textbook in a foreign country and then move to Alabama where people do not speak English. And then, on top of that, my students have to try to learn economics from a guy from Mississippi, which has the highest illiteracy rates in the country. I should clarify here and say that I am not illiterate; I just choose sometimes not to use correct grammar. Here are a couple of examples.

"Suntnuther" - I have in times past had international students tell me that we people in the South *sing* our words more so than we say our words. English teachers would probably call this "diminished enunciation." So it is with "suntnuther".

"Suntnuther" is a series of words combined to form one. It is literally translated "something or other." I'll use it in a sentence. "I'moan (translated "I am going to") run in the gas station here and get me a Co-Coler (translated Coca-Cola) suntnuther. You want suh-m? (This last sentence should be translated as a hospitable offer to buy the asked individual "something"). The speaker here may indeed get a Coca-Cola Classic or some other brand of soft drink (for they are all called "Coke" in the South), or any number of convenience store items such as potato chips, peanut butter and crackers (called "nabs"), bubble gum, beef jerky, etc. The point here, and it's an important one, is that "suntnuther" encompasses many, many things.

"Yonder" – This is actually a real word. It can be used as an adverb, adjective, or pronoun. Its etymology is 14th century Middle English, from the word *yond* as in *hither*. Webster defines yonder as: "at or in that indicated more or less distant place usually within sight." Is that vague enough for you?

I grew up going to New Prospect Missionary Baptist Church. Often we would sing the old hymn, "When the Roll is Called Up Yonder." There was no vagueness in this song. The "yonder" mentioned was speaking of Heaven, but yonder doesn't always mean Heaven. If you are at

104

home in your living room, yonder could be the bedroom or it could be in the next county over. The word "yonder" encompasses many places.

While "suntnuther" includes many things, and "yonder" includes many places, neither word is as inclusive as the word "all." Our text verse reads, "And we know that in *all* things God works for the good of those who love him, who have been called according to his purpose."

"All things" means everything! "All things" includes broken dishes, and broken windows, and broken bones, and broken hearts and broken dreams and broken lives. "All things" covers disappointments, and despair, and disabilities, and divorce, and disease, and even death. Are all of these things good? No. But the verse here does not say that all things *are* good; it says all things *work* for *the* good. (We'll come back to this later.)

Do you believe that? Do you think that all of the horrible things I just mentioned are truly working together for the greater good? Allow me to quote part of an autobiographical account of an adventure I recently read:

"I have worked much harder, been in prison more frequently, been flogged more severely, and been exposed to death again and again. Five times I received ...the forty lashes minus one.

Three times I was beaten with rods, once I was stoned, three times I was shipwrecked, I spent a night and a day in the open sea, I have been constantly on the move. I have been in danger from rivers, in danger from bandits, in danger from my own countrymen…. in danger in the city, in danger in the country, in danger at sea; and in danger from false brothers. I have labored and toiled and have often gone without sleep; I have known hunger and thirst and have often gone without food;I have been cold and naked. Besides everything else, I face daily the pressure of my concern…"

Do you think the person who lived this series of horrific events believes that "in *all* things God works for good"? I sure do. As a matter of fact, I know he did. How can I be so certain? I am certain because Paul is the author of both. That's right! The same guy that endured all of these things described in 2 Corinthians 11:23-28 also reminds us that "in *all* things," even those terrible things he *experienced*, God himself is working for good. That is amazing faith based on an amazing truth.

God Works for the Good

Long ago I had some friends who owned a pet bird. The bird was known for two things. First, the bird could say, "Whatcha doin'?" The bird would do this unprompted, and the tone of his voice made you believe he truly expected an answer. It was a bit unnerving. The second thing he was known for was his cleanliness. He would periodically climb down from his perch, waddle into the kitchen and proceed to take a bird bath in the dog's water bowl.

One day my friend came home from work and proceeded through the back yard to open the back door so the dog could come inside for awhile to escape the summer heat. Unbeknownst to her, the bird was in the middle of his bathing ritual when the dog burst inside. When my friend came around the corner into the kitchen, all she could see were the bird's tail feathers hanging out of the dog's mouth, the dog's jaws poked out like Louis Armstrong, and the bird in muffled voice yelling, "Whatcha doin'? Whatcha doin'? Whatcha doin'?"

Do you ever want to ask that of God? Do you ever look to the sky and say, "Lord, what are you doing to me here?" I think it's a legitimate question. As a youngster, I was taught never to question God. I was told it was disrespectful. And in one sense, it can be. If, for example, you shake your fist at Heaven and yell "What are you doing?" implying that God has lost his focus or that he doesn't know what's best, then I think that your questioning is disrespectful.

Actually, your questioning is not even a question. It is a declaration against the Almighty, Creator of the universe. You are in a sense saying, "God you don't know what you're doing!" Consider this from Jeremiah 29:11 – "For I know the plans I have for you," declares the LORD, "plans to prosper you and not to harm you, plans to give you hope and a future." That is a precious promise from God. And God always keeps his promises.

Therefore, I believe it is the attitude with which we question, rather than the questions themselves, that makes a difference. What if something happens in your life that you find disappointing or tragic or confusing or something that absolutely redirects the very core of your existence?

At that point, offer up an honest prayer from a humble heart, something like, "Lord, in your time and in your way, help me to understand how these events will glorify and honor you. Help me to see what it is that you are doing. Help me to see what *is* in spite of what seems to be." I think God hears, and honors, and answers those prayers. Just this morning I heard a pastor on the radio say, "The prayer that gets to Heaven, starts in Heaven. All we do is complete the circuit."

When crazy things happen and you wonder what God is doing, remember this: God is weaving, out of the fabric of our lives, with his needle of truth and thread of grace, a beautiful tapestry for our good.

Of Those Who Love Him,
Who Have Been Called

This is a difficult chapter for me to write. The Apostle Paul tells us in Ephesians 4 verses 14 and 15 that one of the characteristics of a mature follower of Christ is "speaking the truth in love." That's exactly what I want to do here. I want to speak the truth in love. The world today would tell us that there is no such thing as truth or that truth is relative. However, Jesus said "I am the truth" and "I am the same yesterday, today, and forever." So there is our standard.

I recently heard a conversation on the radio between former NBA player Charles Barkley and syndicated talk show host Rick Burgess of the "Rick and Bubba Show." The conversation went something like this. Charles said that he felt compelled to be inclusive when it came to all choices, such as the right to have an abortion or lead a homosexual lifestyle. Rick argued that those choices are wrong. Charles said, "Wrong, according to *you*." Rick answered, "No, wrong according to the one and only living Creator, the Almighty, Jehovah God. It don't make a rip what I, Rick Burgess, believe."

Charles said we shouldn't judge people. Rick said it's not judging when you hold people accountable according to what God has said. Charles then said let God speak for Himself. And Rick said that God has spoken to us through the Word he has given us.

It was an interesting conversation to say the least, especially because of the size of the personalities involved. I came away with several nuggets from that conversation, not the least of which was, "It doesn't matter what I believe." What matters is truth. Sir Charles and many others have become leery of people who call themselves Christians because of the personal spin some have put on religion. Man has messed up religion because man is imperfect. Truth, and perfection, and salvation come from God.

As I began to study this verse, the phrases "Of those who love him" and "who have been called" weighed heavy on my mind. I finally had to ask myself two questions: 1) "If all things are working for the *good* of those who love God, does that mean that all things are working for the *bad* of those who do not love him?", and 2) "Are there some people who have *not* been called?"

The second question is easy enough to answer with Scripture. In Titus 2:11, Paul tells us, "For the grace of God that brings salvation has appeared to *all* men." 2 Peter 3:9 says, "The Lord is not slow in keeping his promise, as some understand slowness. He is patient with you, not wanting *anyone* to perish, but *everyone* to come to repentance"(*emphasis added*).

Paul also writes in Ephesians 1 verses 13 and 14, "And you *also* were included in Christ when you heard the word of truth, the gospel of your salvation. Having believed, you were marked in him with a seal, the promised Holy Spirit, who is a deposit guaranteeing our inheritance until the redemption of those who are God's possession—to the praise of his glory"(*emphasis added*). All have been called. When do we all become included in the called of Christ? After we hear the word of truth. When are we marked with a seal guaranteeing our inheritance? After having believed.

Therein lies the complication. Allow me to use an illustration. I am from the South. Here we pride ourselves on manners and hospitality. In the South we speak to people and make conversation with individuals, some we don't even know. It's just polite. It's just good manners. And if someone speaks to you and you don't speak back, it's just rude. All have been called. All have been spoken to. It's just that some have decided to be rude and not speak back and answer that calling.

Now, back to the first question I asked, which was, "If all things are working for the *good* of those who love God, does that mean that all things are working for the *bad* of those who do not?" The simple answer is "Yes." Apart from personal relationship with Jesus Christ, we are all on a destructive path that leads to the ultimate "bad," which is eternal separation from God in a devil's hell. Proverbs 14:12 says, "There is a way that seems right to a man, but in the end it leads to death."

How could a loving God sentence someone, anyone, to an eternal death? Doesn't God love everyone? Absolutely, he does. He loves us just as we are, but he loves us too much to let us stay just as we are. He is a God of mercy, a God of grace, a God of love, but also a God of justice. And justice is a good thing. When someone is raped, or murdered, or kidnapped, or done some other wrong, our hearts cry out for justice.

Our God is a just God, and because of our sins, we have all fallen short of his glorious standard. A crime has been committed. A debt must be paid. Jesus has paid that debt once, for all. God has deemed that sacrifice acceptable and in complete fulfillment of all that is required. The only question now is whether or not we will accept Jesus' payment for us or choose to pay the penalty ourselves. That to me seems, as the young people say, a "no-brainer."

2 Timothy 4:3 warns us, "For the time will come when men will not put up with sound doctrine. Instead, to suit their own desires, they

will gather around them a great number of teachers to say what their itching ears want to hear." Let us not fall into this trap. Let us never decide what we believe to be, and then afterwards check to see if the Bible agrees with our feelings.

Instead, may we, as Paul continues to encourage in Ephesians 4, reach for the knowledge of the Son of God and become mature so that we will no longer be tossed back and forth by the waves and blown here and there by every wind of teaching.

According to His Purpose

There are some big questions in life. Why am I here? What am I supposed to do with my life? Can I make a difference? There are also some smaller, yet still significant questions. Where should I go to school? What should I major in? Whom should I marry? Should I marry at all? Should I take this job? Should I relocate? All of us have asked these questions, or some similar, at some point in our lives. When I began to ponder these issues in my own life, I became frustrated and confused. Then I realized I was just asking the wrong questions.

Many years ago, I read in one of Max Lucado's books, "God's main objective is not to make you happy; it's to make you His!" How profound. How true. Ever since the fall of man, and the one fruit fiasco in the Garden of Eden, God has been about the business of calling his children back to Himself. Everything that has occurred between that point in time and this one, has been coordinated to point people to the Father and bring glory and honor to Him.

I have heard people say, "God wouldn't want me to be unhappy." Where does this kind of reasoning end? "God wouldn't want me to be unhappy at this university, so I'll transfer somewhere else. God wouldn't want me to be unhappy in this job, so I'll quit and see if I can find one somewhere else. God wouldn't want me to be unhappy in this marriage, so I'll get divorced and find someone else. God wouldn't want me to be unhappy with these children, so I'll strap them in their car seats and run the vehicle into a river." It's faulty logic. Max was right. God's main objective is to make you His.

I think this is the first step in our quest towards answering life's big questions. We must realize that everything is not working out for our purposes, but according to His purpose. His sole purpose. His one and only purpose is to bring glory to Himself. Why? Because He deserves it! But, you might ask, doesn't God want me to be happy? Well, yes and no.

He wants you to be happy, but He's not willing to compromise his purpose for your party. (I love a man of principle!) Jesus himself said in John 10:10, "I have come that they may have life, and have it to the full." A full life sounds like happiness to me. The key is to allow his purpose to become our purpose. Romans 12:2 reminds us, "Do not conform any longer to the pattern of this world, but be *transformed* by the renewing of your mind. Then you will be able to test and approve what God's will is—his good, pleasing and perfect will" (*emphasis added*).

Sometimes we say, "God show us your will." I fear that oftentimes what we mean by that is, "I'll take a look at it and decide if it suits me." We must completely surrender. You might say to yourself, if I turn my life over to God, if I trade my purposes for His purpose, then He'll ship me off to be a missionary in deepest, darkest Africa. That may be true. Yet, while there you will realize that there is no better place than smack dab in the middle of God's will for your life.

So many times I hear Christians and non-Christians alike say, "Everything happens for a reason." And they are exactly right. However, very rarely, if ever, do they say what that reason is. Well, now you know. The reason is for God's purpose. Will there be personal disappointments? Sure, there will. But we must remember that there is a bigger picture involved. Eternal consequences are at stake.

Everything is designed to bring you (and all people for that matter) closer to the God who loves you. "And we know that in all things God works for the good of those who love him, who have been called according to his purpose." Wow, what a verse!

Two Little Words

Introduction

I am intrigued with words and the English language. I enjoy telling a good story that makes people laugh. I like presenting ideas and theories to my students that make them think and ponder. I am thrilled with the opportunities presented by a blank page inviting an author to create something from nothing. I love words because of their power to invoke a response. The best words and writing are those that make us feel something. That emotion could be happiness or anger or sadness or loathing or regret. Words intrigue me, and I think I know part of the reason why.

I, for obvious reasons, have had to deal with some limitations my entire life. It has certainly been easier to cope with my cerebral palsy as an adult than it was as a child. The first reason for this has mostly to do with the physical aspect of things. Getting dressed, transferring into and out of a vehicle, and even preparing to eat a bowl of cereal present their own unique set of challenges to a person in a wheelchair. And so we learn from experience. Dealing with a disability, one must always be prepared to "improvise, adapt, and overcome." With experience comes knowing the best and worst ways to do things.

The second reason that dealing with a disability is easier as an adult than as a child is, that as an adult, I can "accept the things I cannot change" more quickly than when I was seven or ten. I think it is an issue less about mental capacity and more about perspective. As a kid, I would look around and see other kids doing so much that I could not do. As an adult, however, my foolish pride allows me to notice things that I can do better than others.

One scenario that repeated itself over and again as I was growing up, was at family holidays and other get-togethers, all the kids would run outside to play. Either I would be left behind to gather my crutches and slowly try to make my way to where they were, or I would be left behind all together. I would be "stuck inside with the grown-ups." Little did I know, during those times, what a profound impact this would have on my life. It was indeed a blessing in disguise.

During my imprisonment with the adults, they would just sit around and talk. How boring is that! Well, maybe not as boring as you might think. There were some great story tellers in my family. Both my grandfathers could "spin a yarn." My Uncle Burt, the best man at my parent's wedding, and my Great-Uncle Prent, after whom my son is named, both kept us laughing with their stories. Even Mom's first cousin Jeanine could tell stories like the old folks.

And so I learned from the best. I soon realized that, while I might not get attention as a child by scoring a run in T-ball or building a great tree house, I could make people laugh by telling jokes. I remember as a young child not telling knock-knocks or one-liners, but jokes with set-up, characters, and punch-lines. People love to laugh, and it seemed they loved me more when I made them laugh.

So I learned to love words. I love words because they can make us feel something, and I love words because they can change your life. Here are some four word phrases that can change your life: "Dad is coming home," "Your house burned down," and "Will you marry me?" There are also some three word phrases that have profound impact, things like "It's a girl," "Your new car," or "I love you." There are even some single words that carry a huge amount of weight in and of themselves, such as "Cancer," "Hurricane," or "Goodbye."

I have found a two word phrase, however, that changes things more radically than all others put together. This phrase is used many times in the Bible in lots of different situations. It is penetrating, uplifting, encouraging and powerful. It is the phrase, "*But God.*"

Do Dead People Bleed?

The Book of Ephesians, Chapter 2 begins, "As for you, you were dead in your transgressions and sins, in which you used to live when you followed the ways of this world and of the ruler of the kingdom of the air, the spirit who is now at work in those who are disobedient. All of us also lived among them at one time, gratifying the cravings of our sinful nature and following its desires and thoughts. Like the rest, we were by nature objects of wrath."

It's a bit depressing. First, we are told we were dead. Let me tell you a story about being dead. It comes from a psychiatrist dealing with the criminally insane at a maximum security prison. He had a patient who believed himself dead. There was no reasoning with the man. Never mind that he was walking among the living; in his mind, he truly believed he was no longer alive.

The doctor, in an effort to counsel the inmate, asked, "Do dead people bleed?" The inmate assured his counselor that dead people certainly did not bleed. Then the doctor asked if it be okay if a nurse came in and pricked the patient's finger to be sure that he was dead. "After all," the doctor said, "We can't have a dead person walking around scaring other inmates who are already mentally unstable." The dead man consented.

The nurse came in, his finger was pricked,

and amazingly a crimson liquid oozed from the small opening. Starring incredulously at his finger the inmate announced, "Well, I'll be! Dead people *do* bleed!"

Do you know what is worse than being alive, yet thinking you are dead? It is thinking you are alive, yet in truth being dead. Ever since the fall of man in the Garden of Eden, the human race has found itself dead and dying. Verse 1 of this chapter says "you were dead in your transgressions and sins." And in case you think the writer is not talking to you, Paul continues in verse 3 by saying "all of us".

God is a holy God. He has set a standard that will not be compromised. We are separated from God because of our disobedience (verse 2). If left to satisfy our own cravings and follow our sinful desires and thoughts (verse 3), we will reap the consequences of that disobedience. Romans 6:23 could not be more clear or concise when it states that the consequence is death.

I'm so glad I don't have to stop writing here. That would be hopeless indeed. So far the only redeeming quality about the passage in question is that it is written in past tense. That means something had to change. What changed was the introduction of my favorite two-word phrase, "But God." Ephesians 2:4-5 says, "*But God*, who is rich in mercy, because of His great love with which He loved us, even when we were dead in trespasses, made us alive together with Christ (by grace you have been saved)"(*emphasis added*). (NKJV)

If that don't crank your tractor, then your starter must be broke! This is the great roadblock on our way to an eternal Hell, separated from God! Christians use the phrase "I am saved" to indicate their acceptance of Jesus' perfect sacrifice on the cross as the required penalty God says must be paid for their sins. We must first, however, be convinced that we are drowning in sin. It is only after that realization we will ever acknowledge that if we are alive, it is not because we learned how to swim! We have been rescued, and this verse is the life-preserver!

The first word of this amazing two-word phrase does not usually carry with it a positive connotation. A parent may say to a teenager, "You may go to the movies, *but* you must take your little brother with you." A boyfriend may say to his girlfriend, "I love you, *but* I cannot marry you." The word "but" is generally followed by bad news. Not in this case. "But God" changes things in the most positive way possible. It says despite everything you've done and everything that you should suffer because of it, God has intervened. The Lord of all creation has stepped into the picture and given us a way out.

Why does God do this? Verses 6 and 7 tell

us. "And God raised us up with Christ and seated us with him in the heavenly realms in Christ Jesus, *in order that* in the coming ages he might show the incomparable riches of his grace, expressed in his kindness to us in Christ Jesus" *(emphasis added)*. Isn't that amazing! As if it were not enough to learn about the extraordinary power contained in the phrase "But God", now we have "*And* God".

As if it were not enough that he saved us, now he tells us why. It's so he could show us how rich he is! And as Paul Bryant said, "It ain't braggin' if you can back it up." Not only do we learn in verse four that God is rich in mercy, but now in verse seven we see that He is rich in grace as well. Do you know the difference?

I've been taught that mercy is *not* getting something *bad* you deserve, and grace is getting something *good* that you *don't* deserve. These verses tell us God is rich in both. He is rich in mercy in that because of our sins we deserve death, and yet he provided a means of escape. He is rich in grace in that he freely gives his children an eternal home in paradise, something we could never earn on our own. Who couldn't love a God like that?

Not of Noble Birth

I am not a medical doctor, so my knowledge of this disability outside of personal experience is very limited. I know that in my particular case, cerebral palsy was caused by complications during birth. I was born breech, and oxygen was delayed getting to the part of the brain known as the cerebellum, hence the name. CP is not progressive, meaning the brain damage will not get worse, but other difficulties, such as premature arthritis or curvature of the spine, are common.

Those with CP are sometimes stigmatized and shunned. There was a time the great majority of people with CP were often sent to asylums or confined to attics. They were perceived to be the products of incest and partial smothering. Often parents kept their children away from them in the mistaken belief that the condition was the product of disease or poor sanitary habits. Until the 1970s, doctors believed there was a correlation between physical disability and aptitude, and a common misunderstanding then and now is that CP causes mental retardation.

First Corinthians 1:26 reads, "Brothers, think of what you were when you were called. Not many of you were wise by human standards; not many were influential; not many were of noble birth." Have you ever felt this way? I certainly fall into that category. After I was born, even though my mother insisted something was wrong, I was sent home from the hospital like any other child. I was very healthy, remarked the doctor. As my parents realized I was not physically progressing properly, not rolling over or crawling at the appropriate age, they took me to an orthopedic specialist, where I was diagnosed with cerebral palsy. He told my parents not expect too much, because, again, CP was thought to be linked to mental retardation.

There is no known cure for cerebral palsy.

Once again two little words come in to play, "But God". Verses twenty-seven and twenty-eight interrupt, "*But God* chose the foolish things of the world to shame the wise; God chose the weak things of the world to shame the strong. He chose the lowly things of this world and the despised things—and the things that are not—to nullify the things that are" *(emphasis added)*. Wow, how those words change things.

Why does God choose to do things this way? Verse twenty-nine gives us the answer: "So that no one may boast before him." Never forget this; everything is to glorify Him (not us), because He alone is worthy. One of the many blessings of my disability - yes, you're reading that correctly -

is that I learned at a very early age how many things I could not do on my own.

As Americans, so many of us are taught the "protestant work ethic." We should work hard, and when things go wrong, we should pull ourselves up by our own bootstraps. I am in no way knocking hard work. However, we must realize that there are things beyond our control, and there are times we must lean on something larger than ourselves.

Later, in the fifteenth chapter and tenth verse of this same book, Paul writes, "But by the grace of God I am what I am, and his grace to me was not without effect. No, I worked harder than all of them—yet not I, but the grace of God that was with me." What inner peace to be able to say, "I am what I am." I am what I am because the god in "But God" is "the Great I Am."

Just Drink the Kool-Aid

The seventh chapter of the Book of Acts is mostly a manuscript of Stephen's speech to the Sanhedrin. He gives them a thumbnail sketch of the history of the Jewish people. Let me remind you here that he's talking to Jewish people here who should *already* know their history. The irony is precisely the point. Stephen basically asked them how they could crucify the Savior that God had sent them, after all that God had done for his people. Then they stone him.

As he begins, verses nine through ten read, "Because the patriarchs were jealous of Joseph, they sold him as a slave into Egypt. *But God* was with him and rescued him from all his troubles. He gave Joseph wisdom and enabled him to gain the goodwill of Pharaoh King of Egypt; so he made him ruler over Egypt and all his palace" (*emphasis added*). So many things are changed by these two little words, "But God."

First of all, can you imagine your brothers being so jealous of you that they sell you into slavery? Talk about your sibling rivalry! But the amazing thing here is that what his brothers intended for evil, God intended for good (Genesis 50:20). In the long run, Joseph rescues his entire family because of his position. It is simply an amazing turn of events. Read the whole story in Genesis thirty seven through forty-seven.

Acts 7:9-10 gives us a brief glimpse into this tremendous story. First of all it tells of God's presence: "God was with him." What blessed assurance to know that the Lord of all the earth is alive and active in our everyday lives. Next, we see God's deliverance, "and rescued him from all his troubles." Notice this verse does not say that God prevented the troubles from happening.

Sometimes God allows us to go through difficult circumstances to guide us to the place where we will do the greatest good, and He will be most glorified. Third we read that God "gave Joseph wisdom." Psalm 111:10 states, "The fear of the LORD is the beginning of wisdom..." Finally our verse states that Joseph grew in favor with God and man as he "gains the goodwill of Pharaoh King of Egypt; so he made him ruler over Egypt and all his palace." Now, personally, I believe that man does not bestow power, but what first God grants him.

Are you convinced yet? Have you, as the young people say, "drank the Kool-Aid?" Do you really believe that there is no circumstance that is so desperate that the phrase "But God" will not drastically change things for the better? Add those two little words to each of the following:

I've run out of hope....

I can't figure this out....

Everyone else does it....

I'm at the end of my rope....

I just can't hold on any longer....

I need a drink or a fix....

I need a romantic relationship....

I'm tired; I quit. I can't....

I've given all I can give, and it's just not enough....

But God! But God loved the world so much...that he did something about it. That is the good news that we should be sharing.

It's a Family Thang

Elasticity, Practicality and Mom

Almost always at the beginning of a semester, I will ask my collegiate students what they expect to learn in my class. Often I will have answers such as "money," "markets," "inflation," and "unemployment." I will also get the occasional "supply and demand" answer. While it is true that we discuss supply and demand in every section of classes that I teach, in my Microeconomics classes we examine things a little more closely.

For example: In general, when discussing the concept of demand, economist will explain that there is an inverse relationship between price and quantity demanded. This means that as the price of a good increases, you and I as consumers will tend to buy less of it. Price goes up. Quantity demanded goes down. Easy enough. I remind my students, though, to think about Microeconomics like analyzing something under a "micro"-scope. In this class, we examine individual businesses and markets with a fine-toothed comb, so to speak.

Under the microscope, we get down to the nitty-gritty and ask more pointed questions. Sure, if price goes up, quantity demanded goes down, but the question becomes "*how much?*" In other words, if a business owner raises the price of his or her product, does the quantity demanded go down a little, or a lot? This concept is explained in Economic jargon with vocabulary called "elasticity." If the demand for a product is *very* responsive to changes in price, we say that it is "elastic." However, if it is *not very* responsive to changes in price the terminology is "inelastic."

I use a story about my mother to illustrate the point. Several years ago around the holidays, Mom asked me what I needed for Christmas. (When you get to be my age, mothers don't ask what you *want* for Christmas.) I told her that I could use some slacks to wear to work. She asked what size I wore. I said, "I wear a 32, but a 34 feels *so* good, I just go ahead and get a 36." Do you know what Mom bought me? Old man pants... with elastic in the waist! I call them my "Thanksgiving pants" because they *respond* when I eat.

Given the information she had, this was the most practical thing my mother could do. And Mom is nothing if not practical. I realize that some people stereotype the female of our species as flighty and irrational. In fact, in one of the more memorable lines from the 1997 movie *As Good As It Gets*, Jack Nicholson's character responds to the question "how do you write women so well?" by saying, "I think of a man...and I take away reason and accountability." This could not be further from the truth about my mother. Mom is one of the most logical women I know.

Mom tells the story that when I started to kindergarten someone saw me struggling to walk on my crutches and offered to carry me inside the school. Mom explained that I needed to learn to do things on my own because one day I would be too big for someone else to carry. So began my journey towards independence, and I have Mom, in large part, to thank for that. She taught me how to be organized, and how to balance a checkbook, and many of the other logical, practical character traits that I posses today.

So, in honor of my Mom, I want to pass along to you some of the most practical advice ever uttered. Romans 12:1 says, "I beseech you therefore, brethren, by the mercies of God, that you present your bodies a living sacrifice, holy, acceptable to God, which is your reasonable service."(NKJV) Let's pick this verse apart for a moment. Shall we?

- **I beseech you** – I urge. I ask. I beg of you to do this thing

- *Therefore* – I was taught long ago, that when studying the Bible, and you see the word "therefore", you should always ask yourself, "What is this 'therefore' *there for*?" This one is pretty easy. The

Apostle Paul, the writer of the Book of Romans, has just spent eleven chapters trying to show the reader just a glimpse of who God is and what He's been up to. I think this "therefore" is Paul's way of saying, "OK. I've told you all that, to tell you this!"

- **Brethren** – Brothers and sisters in Christ. Folks who have invited Jesus into the heart to be their Lord and Savior.

- **By the mercies of God** – In light of how good, and gracious, and loving and merciful the God I've spent the last eleven chapters telling you about is...

- **That you present your bodies a *living sacrifice*, holy, acceptable to God** – Do you know the problem with living sacrifices? They can crawl off the alter when the flames get too high. That is why Jesus said in Luke 9:23, "Whoever wants to be my disciple *must deny themselves* and *take up their cross daily* and follow me"(*emphasis added*).

- **Which is your *reasonable* service** – Why? Why would you offer yourself as a sacrifice? Why would you deny yourself? Why would you take up a bloody cross every day? Why? Well, Paul says it's just the reasonable thing to do! What? Are you kidding me? It's crazy talk, right?

The short answer is no. It's not crazy at all. If God is who He says He is (emphasis on the sovereignty of God), and He'll do what He said He'll do (emphasis on the promises of God), then the only thing that makes any sense at all is to submit all that we have and all that we are to Him. It's reasonable. It's logical. It's practical. Just like my Mom.

Daddy's Little Girl

I call my daughter "Ladybug". At this writing she is nine months old, "no bigger than a minute" and desperately attempting to walk. She watches her big brother run around the house like a mad man, and you can see in her eyes that she wants in on the action. She's "quicker than a hiccup" when crawling, especially towards any open door. She's been "couch surfing" for quite awhile. But this walking thing sometimes gives her fits! (I know. I know. Justin, who are you to criticize someone's walking ability?)

The trick, it seems, to a child's learning to walk, is learning to let go. Let go of that couch. Let go of that book shelf. Let go of that footstool. Let go of that toy that will roll while you push it while learning to walk. But letting go is scary. If I let go I might fall. I think I'll just hold on a little longer. Or better yet, I think I'll just crawl some more. I'm pretty good at that.

Well, if you've read this far in this book, you know where this is going. Letting go isn't just challenging for toddlers. It's pretty tricky for adults as well. Notice what Paul says in Philippians 3:7-9 &12 about the things he's let go of:

"But whatever were *gains to me* I now consider *loss for the sake of Christ*. What is more, I consider *everything a loss* because of the surpassing worth of knowing Christ Jesus my Lord, for whose sake *I have lost all things*. I consider them garbage, that I may gain Christ. Not that I have already obtained all this, or have already arrived at my goal, but I press on *to take hold of that for which Christ Jesus took hold of me*" (*emphasis added*).

Following Christ may indeed cost you something. To follow Christ you may have to lose some things. He may even ask you to leave some things that you consider very important to you. Jesus says in Matthew 10:37-39, "Anyone who loves their father or mother more than me is not worthy of me; anyone who loves their son or daughter more than me is not worthy of me. Whoever does not take up their cross and follow me is not worthy of me. Whoever finds their life will lose it, and whoever loses their life for my sake will find it."

Yeah, you may have to let go of something or some things, but what you gain pales in comparison to what you've lost. So let go, Ladybug. Let go! And let us all learn this lesson as well.

MY Grandmommy

Kelly's grandmother is named Pauline
Williams. She goes by several names, however,
including Mom, Mrs. Pauline, and Aunt Polly; but
she was introduced to me at the age of 91 as
simply "Grandmommy." Kelly and I had been
"seriously dating" for some time, and I was invited
to Hiram, Georgia, to spend the weekend and get
to know the family. The first time I ever met
Grandmommy, she hugged my neck and said,
"Don't they have any pretty girls where you're
from?" It was like I'd known her all my life, and
so began a wonderful relationship.

Grandmommy and I get along for several
reasons, but I think the primary reason is because I
like to talk and Grandmommy loves a good story.
She has been a tremendous encouragement to me
during the writing of this book. She is a saintly
woman of God who loves Jeopardy, great-
grandchildren, and chocolate.

One day, the family was sitting around
chatting and the subject of re-incarnation came up.
Grandmommy said, "You know I don't believe in
that stuff, but if I did I think I'd probably come
back as a wolf." Well, you can imagine the

chuckles that ensued. "Why do you think you'd come back as a wolf?" someone asked. "Well, I guess, it's 'cause I'm so mean" Grandmommy replied.

She then went on to recount for us a story from her childhood. She said that when she was a little girl in school, one of her classmates was from "the wrong side of the tracks." Grandmommy said they would throw rocks at the girl and tease her about her father making moonshine. "I don't know if that was true about her Daddy, but that was the story anyway." You could tell in Grandmommy's voice that there was a twinge of guilt about how she had treated another human being even after eighty plus years.

Trying to lighten the mood a bit, Cousin Jo-Jo said, "Pauline, you know how Justin tells stories, he'll probably be telling that about you." Grandmommy simply smiled and said, "Well, maybe so, but I'm gonna die and go to Heaven before he does, and I'll tell God it ain't true!"

So much to learn, from that story in particular, and from Grandmommy in general. I'm sure that the teasing carried about by Grandmommy and her posse was part of harmless child's play, but again, you could tell it bothered her just a bit. Why? Because Grandmommy knows what I'm trying to learn and put into practice; everyone is made in the image of God and because of that they all have dignity. Picture the lowest, low-life, scum sucking, varmit of a human being you can think of, and they are still closer to God than anything else on the planet because they are made in His image. I dare say that the biggest regret most of us will have when we stand before the judgment seat of Christ is the way we have treated His children.

Grandmommy is ninety-six at this writing. She has already begun dropping hints that she might not be around much longer. She doesn't say it with any hint of sadness, though. But that's what happens when you have an intimacy with the One you know you'll spend eternity with. Jesus says in John 14:2-3, "My Father's house has many rooms; if that were not so, would I have told you that I am going there to prepare a place for you? And if I go and prepare a place for you, I will come back and take you to be with me that you also may be where I am."

Pop's Watch

I didn't know wife's father, Danny Williams, nearly long enough. He died of brain cancer just a little over two years after we married. My children will never know their Pop. That saddens me, but not nearly as much as it does Kelly I'm sure. Pop and I did share some good times before he passed. Let me share a couple with you.

The first time I went with Kelly to visit her family, Danny took me deer hunting. (I realize that going out into the woods with loaded weapons with a man whose daughter you are dating might not be the smartest decision. But I figured he didn't know me well enough to dislike me too much). I climbed the steps to his lakeside cabin using my crutches and he offered me his room to use to change into my hunting clothes. As we prepared to leave, Pop walked out of the front door ahead of me. The door was designed to swing closed after anyone exited, and so it did, right in my face. You can imagine how physically challenging it is to open a swinging door and maneuver through it while walking on crutches. Danny's best friend, Matt, was sitting on the couch, saw my dilemma and offered to help. Matt said, "I guess he thinks you can walk through doors... Although if you're going to marry his daughter, you better be able to walk on water, too."

A few weeks later, I called Danny to officially ask him for Kelly's hand in marriage. He said, "Sure. She's a good girl. We never had a bit of trouble out of her." Then I said, "I want you to know that I'll do my best to take care of her and make her happy." To which he replied, "Well, if you make her happy, you'll be doing better than any of the rest of us ever have." Kelly's mom and sister love that story!

Danny was a fairly wealthy man who built his own construction and real estate development businesses, pardon the pun, from the ground up. Before he passed away, Pop gave me his watch. It's a Rolex; a timepiece I could never purchase myself. If anyone ever compliments me on it, I am quick to point out that it was, indeed, a gift. Our Heavenly Father has also given us a gift we could never afford. Romans 5:15-17 says, "But the *gift* is not like the trespass. For if the many died by the trespass of the one man (Adam), how much more did God's grace and the *gift* that came by the grace of the one man, Jesus Christ, overflow to the many! Nor can the *gift* of God be compared with the result of one man's sin: The judgment followed one sin and brought condemnation, but the *gift* followed many trespasses and brought justification. For if, by the trespass of the one man, death reigned through that one man, how much more will those who receive God's abundant provision of grace and of the *gift* of righteousness reign in life through the one man, Jesus Christ!" (*emphasis added*).

What's Keepin' Ya?

My favorite movie of all time is actually not a movie at all. It's a mini-series that aired in the late '80s called *Lonesome Dove*. It stars Tommy Lee Jones and Robert Duvall as former Texas Rangers on a cattle drive to Montana. Jones' character is Woodrow Call, a tough-as-nails, no nonsense, straightforward, workaholic type. On the other hand, Gus McCrae, played by Duvall, is a philosophical, practical joker, ladies man. It's kind of like *The Odd Couple* set in the Old West.

Just as they're about to leave on the drive, they have a conversation that goes something like this:

Woodrow: Well, the fun's all over down here.

Gus: What do you mean "fun?" *Fun* is my department. And I think now I'll ride into town and see if I can't scare me up a little bit of it.

Woodrow: We've got all we can handle right here without you ridin' off into town.

Gus: Well I'm just tryin' to keep everything in balance. See, you do more work than you've got to, so it's my obligation to do *less*!

And with that, Gus spurs his horse and rides off toward town.

Woodrow (*calling out after Gus*): Hey! We got a herd of cattle to look after.

Gus (*without looking back*): Well, what's keepin' ya?

That's my question to you today. What's keeping you? During the Christmas season, I hear many people say things like: "I want Christmas to be different this year." "I don't want to rush through the Holidays, just to be exhausted at the end." "I want to take time to remember the true reason for the season this Christmas." I must confess that I've had these exact same thoughts and feeling. My response, however, is the same as Gus's: "What's keeping you?" This requires some thought, some honesty, some introspection. We read in the Bible of another group who missed Christmas; seeing who and why might aid in evaluating our own predicament and keeping us from making the same mistake.

Matthew 2:4-6 reads, "When (Herod) had called together all the people's chief priests and teachers of the law, he asked them where the Messiah was to be born. "In Bethlehem in Judea," they replied, "for this is what the prophet has written: "'But you, Bethlehem, in the land of Judah, are by no means least among the rulers of Judah; for out of you will come a ruler who will shepherd my people Israel.'"

In short, Herod called in the experts. The chief priests would have had great administrative, teaching and leadership skills. The teachers of the law, also called scribes, would have been interpreters that specialized in languages, and cultures, and the historical nature of Biblical data.

Do you know what kept them from Christmas? Quite simply, they didn't care. Oh, they were smart, alright. You would have been hard pressed to find a group of more educated people on the planet at the time. They had all the details, all the facts, all the data, but they didn't think they needed the Son of God. In their minds, they had kept the law perfectly. And you don't need a Savior if you don't even know what it is that you're being saved from.

Many people in our day are rowing the same boat. They refuse to grab hold of the life preserver because they don't even know they're drowning. They miss Christmas because, even though they know *that* Jesus came, they don't know *why* He had to come in the first place. He came to save us from our sins (Matthew 1:21).

Those of you with children know that they tend to learn things from other children, especially older children. My two year-old is no different.

After spending time with his older cousins, he recently came home with the phrase, "I just fine." You might think this sentence cute coming from a two year-old, but he uses it inappropriately. Imagine entering a room, smelling a foul odor, and realizing the odor is coming from the child's diaper.

Parent: "Let's go change your diaper."

Child: "I just fine."

Parent: "No, son. You are not 'just fine.' You have poo-poo in your diaper!"

Child: "I just fine."

Or imagine sitting at the table with this child as he enjoys cereal for a mid-afternoon snack. The boy is rubbing both eyes with the backs of his hands, and is obviously so sleepy you're afraid he might drown in his Cocoa Fruity Pebbles.

Parent: "Let's go take a nap."

Child (*whining*): "I just fine."

Parent: "No, son. You are not 'just fine.' You're about to stab yourself in the eye with your own spoon!"

Child (*crying full force*): "I just fine."

The truth is, dear friend, we are not "just fine" either, and the consequences of our indifference have much greater implications than soiled pants or spoiled nap-times. Until we realize the depth of our depravity, the utter hopelessness of our situation without Jesus, we'll miss Christmas.

Until we acknowledge our sin, admit that our efforts of goodness fall well short of God's holy standard, and accept Jesus, born in that stable long ago, as King of our lives, we'll miss Christmas. We might gather with friends and loved ones, eat a big meal, get some nice presents, enjoy the decorations, but we'll miss Christmas. Well...what's keepin' ya?

Wisdom From Dad

Often times when you go on an outing to a lake or river, you will see a family water skiing. More often than not you will see the dad driving the boat while the children ski. The kids will jump waves, do flips, and perform maneuvers all while dad drives straight. That's what my Dad did. Nothing flashy. Nothing fancy. He just drove straight. He got up every morning before dawn, ate breakfast, and went to a blue collar factory job to earn money to pay the bills. We were never rich, but my siblings and I never worried whether or not our basic needs would be met. This is something that I have long taken for granted, and now realize that many children do not have this luxury.

Dad is a man of few words. But the words he did say were often profound. He said things like, "A willful waste is a woeful want," and "Better to build a small fire and huddle close than to waste much wood and keep backing up." One of Dad's favorite scripture passages is James 4:13-15. It reads, "Now listen, you who say, "Today or tomorrow we will go to this or that city, spend a year there, carry on business and make money." Why, you do not even know what will happen tomorrow. What is your life? You are a mist that appears for a little while and then vanishes.

Instead, you ought to say, "*If it is the Lord's will, we will live and do this or that.*"(*emphasis added*)

I remember once when I was a young boy, my father taking me and my brother fishing. We were notorious for getting our hooks caught in fallen trees and stumps lurking just beneath the water of our small pond. Once when we had accomplished this amazing feat, Dad decided he was going to retrieve the hook, line and sinker rather than using his pocket knife and starting over. Using the tractor, he backed a small trailer out into the water by the fallen tree. To my young eyes he looked like an acrobat, then a tight-rope walker, as he climbed over the back of the tractor seat, balanced on the hitch, then the trailer tongue, and shimmied out to get our fishing supplies.

Once they were retrieved, Dad quickly realized the tractor had become stuck in the mud. Not only was it stuck, but it was situated in such a way that it appeared that any attempt to move it forward was to entertain the possibility that it would turn over sideways into the water. Again, in a maneuver that seemed super-human to me as a child; my Dad drove the tractor at a 45 degree angle over a stump, out of the water all while balancing precariously on a fallen tree. Simply amazing!

"That's *my Dad* who got that tractor unstuck!," I yelled, to no one in particular. Then, with a facial expressed that insured that I understood the peril and gravity of the situation, Dad said, "That's *my God* that kept it from turning over." This was Dad's way of quoting scripture. 2 Corinthians 3:5 says, "Not that we are competent in ourselves to claim anything for ourselves, but our competence comes from God." It was a teachable moment. One I will never forget.

Dad taught me that we do not know what the future holds, yet we know who holds the future, and we know whose hand we hold. And I will pass these teachings on to my children...if it is the Lord's will.

Just
Thrown In

All Things to All Men

While enduring one of the most personally challenging times of my life, my home church of Valleydale moved onto its new campus. During a dedication ceremony, the congregation was invited to write messages of hope or pledge on the concrete foundation before the flooring was installed. Unable to reach the floor from my wheelchair, I asked a good friend to write, among other things, Isaiah 6:8 which reads, "Then I heard the voice of the Lord saying, "Whom shall I send? And who will go for us?" And I said, "Here am I. Send me!" The time recently came for me to make good on that promise.

Containing 21 million residents, serving as the media capital of the world, housing the United Nations center and home to 130 colleges and universities, the metro New York community is arguably the city that most radically impacts the events of our world today. Valleydale launched a partnership with a new church - Encounter Church - whose epicenter would be in the Greenwich and Stamford suburbs in the southernmost part of Connecticut.

The significance of this area is that it is home to many of the societal leaders who influence not simply New York and the U.S. but, in fact, the entire world. I, along with two other guys from church, continued that partnership by taking a mission trip to Stamford in an effort to demonstrate the attractive nature of our God and His gospel. We were able to plant seeds and touch lives in that area of the globe, knowing that we may never know, this side of Heaven, the enormous impact that our going would have on God's Kingdom.

Still, I knew the group would incur greater costs from providing an adapted rental van to carry my power wheelchair and an additional handicapped accessible room. The rental van was of special concern as one cannot simply stop by Hertz or Avis and pick one up, and they're more costly. I didn't want to be a burden.

But my friend Saint Green (yes, that's his real name) reminded me that the eternal God of the universe had formed this team Himself, and these accommodations weren't burdens, but opportunities for ministry. A few short months later, I was sitting on a plane bound for Connecticut.

The major task we were asked to perform by the pastor of Encounter, Landon Reesor, was to distribute gift bags to businesses in the downtown shopping area surrounding the church. Encounter was using the facilities of Calvary Baptist church to hold its services on Sunday evenings. Calvary was built in 1878, but Encounter had only been in town three weeks. The gift bags were an effort to let the community know that there was a Bible based Christian church right down the street that cared about people and wanted to help them draw closer to the God that loves them.

Before one can distribute gift bags, one must first create gift bags. Landon had purchased a van load of candies, mints, cookies and gum. The assembly was up to us. I must admit that three men from Birmingham, Alabama would probably not be anyone's first choice to make up "fru-fru, We're In the Neighborhood" gift bags. However, in 1 Corinthians 9:22 Paul writes, "To the weak I became weak, to win the weak. I have become all things to all men so that by all possible means I might save some." Therefore, we became gift bag makers.

As the assembly line started, our first task was to flare open all of the bags to prepare them to receive the goodies. This went smoothly for the first ten minutes or so, but we then discovered several of the bags were not sealed properly at the bottom. All the contents would fall straight through. I promptly discarded the first few, feeling they were no longer useful and not worth the effort to repair. However, the discards became so numerous that the team decided that it would be wasteful to throw them all away.

I went to the hotel front desk and asked to borrow some tape. There was a large conference style table in the spacious lobby on which to spread my work. As I began the repairs, I realized that two pieces of tape, one vertical and one horizontal, would make the bottom of the bag hold fast. I only had to repeat this process a few times to realize that the tape on the bottom of the bag was making the shape of a cross.

Isn't that a wonderful picture of the Gospel? Jesus draws unto Himself all who are weary, burdened, broken, and cast away as useless to the world. Through the power of the Cross, He repairs our hearts and heals our wounds. He makes us stronger than we ever were before. He prepares us to receive amazing things like peace, and joy, and love, so that we in turn may be a blessing to others.

First Corinthians 15:3-4 says, " For what I received I passed on to you as of *first importance: that Christ died for our sins* according to the Scriptures, that he was buried, that he was raised on the third day according to the Scriptures" (*emphasis added*). We must remember that at the center of everything is the Cross.

That's My King
(Thoughts on a sermon by Sam Lockridge)

In the sixteenth chapter of the book of Genesis, verses seven and following it is written, " The angel of the LORD found Hagar near a spring in the desert; it was the spring that is beside the road to Shur. And he said, "Hagar, servant of Sarai, where have you come from, and where are you going?" "I'm running away from my mistress Sarai," she answered. Then the angel of the LORD told her, "Go back to your mistress and submit to her." The angel added, "I will so increase your descendants that they will be too numerous to count." Then in verse thirteen it says, "She gave this name to the Lord who spoke to her: "You are the God who sees me," for she said, "*I have now seen the One who sees me*"(*emphasis added*).

Now we know that God sees us. We know that he is omniscient. We know that He has infinite awareness, understanding, and insight. We know He possesses universal or complete knowledge. I will take for granted that you believe that God sees you. My question is, "Do you see God? Have you *really* seen the God who sees you?" While in college I heard a sermon by Sam Lockridge that gave me just a peephole glimpse of the God who sees me:

In Psalm 19 verses 1 - 3 King David wrote, "The heavens declare the glory of God; the skies proclaim the work of his hands. Day after day they pour forth speech; night after night they display knowledge. There is no speech or language where their voice is not heard." We know that no means of measure can quantify God's limitless love. No far seeing telescope can bring into visibility the fullness of the grace He extends to us.

He's enduringly strong.

He's entirely sincere.

He's eternally steadfast.

He's immortally graceful.

He's imperially powerful.

He's impartially merciful.

He's God's Son.

He's the sinner's Savior

He's the centerpiece of civilization.

He's unique.

He's unparalleled.

He's unprecedented.

I thought that was good theology, but questioned what it had to do with my life right then and there.

He's the key of knowledge.
He's the well-spring of wisdom.

*Oh, that's what it has to do with me
right now. What about my friends
who are still trying to choose a
major?*

He's the loftiest idea in literature.
He's the miracle of modern medicine.
He's the highest personality in
        philosophy.
He's the fundamental doctrine of true
        theology.
He's the best business bureau known to man.
And history truly is his-story, for it
        begins and ends with Him.

*What about all the struggles I'll face
while in college?*

He's the only One able to supply all
of our needs simultaneously.
He provides strength for the struggling.
He provides healing for the hurting.
He provides truth for the tempted and
        the tested.
He discharges debtors.
He delivers the captives.

He defends the feeble.
He yearns for the young.
He regards the aged.
He rewards the diligent.
He uplifts the unfortunate.
And He beautifies the meek.

*How can I keep from worrying about
life after college?*

He is the Master of the mighty.
He is the captain of the conquerors.
He's the head of the heroes.
He's the leader of the legislators.
He's the overseer of the over-comers.
He is the Governor of Governors.
Why? Because He is the Prince of
         Princes.
He is the King of Kings.
He is the Lord of Lords.

His office is manifold.
His promise is sure.
His light is matchless.
His goodness is limitless.
His mercy is everlasting.
His love never changes.
His Word is enough.
His grace is sufficient.

His reign is righteous.
His yoke is easy.
And His burden is light.
I WISH I COULD DESCRIBE HIM
TO YOU!

But He's indescribable.
He's irresistible.
He's incomprehensible.
He's invincible.
The heavens cannot contain Him.
Let alone a man explain Him.
You can't get Him out of your mind.
You can't wash His blood off your
        hands
You can't out live Him,
And you can't live without Him.

The Pharisees couldn't stand Him,
But they found out they couldn't stop
        Him.
Pilate couldn't find any fault in Him,
And the false witnesses couldn't
        agree.
Herod couldn't hurt Him,
Death couldn't handle Him,
And the grave couldn't hold Him!

He always has been,

And He always will be.
He had no predecessor,
And He'll have no successor.
There was no one before Him,
And there will be no one after Him.
You can't impeach Him,
And He's not going to resign!
Why? Because His is the kingdom
and the power and the glory forever
and ever.
                Amen!

That's my King. King Jesus. That's the God
who sees me…and you. And, by the way, of all of
that commentary does not even remotely come
close to describing how great our God is.
Ephesians 3:20-21 says, "Now unto him that is
able to do *exceeding abundantly above all* that we
ask or think, according to the power that worketh
in us, unto him be glory in the church by Christ
Jesus throughout all ages, world without end.
Amen" (*emphasis added*). Do you know my
King? Now that you've gotten a glimpse, you
must ask yourself the same question Pilate asked of
the crowd in Matthew 27:22, "What shall I do then
with Jesus?"

God's Economy

I love my job. I believe that God has gifted me with the ability to teach. God has given me, I believe, not only the ability to convey information but also to make it interesting and memorable for students. I cannot imagine making a living doing anything else. I cannot imagine anything I would enjoy more. One of the first lectures I give in my Economics classes is about the different sectors of the economy and their conflicting goals.

I explain that, on the one hand, we have consumers. That would be you and me. Our goal is to maximize satisfaction. We do this through a process called cost-benefit analysis, CBA. It sounds more complicated than it is. In fact, everyone uses the process several times each day. It's just that we don't call it "CBA." Cost-benefit analysis is the process of comparing the additional cost that I will have to expend because of a decision, versus the additional benefit I will get to enjoy because of that same decision. An example would be when Kelly and I went on our honeymoon cruise. My travel agent said that we could book a room in the bowels of the ship for one price, or get one with a balcony view for $1,000 more. (My initial question was something about whether these two rooms were on the same ship going to the same places!) I had to decide whether the additional benefit of sitting on the balcony and sipping hot chocolate and watching Hubbard Glacier calve off into the ocean was worth the additional cost of $1,000.

On the other hand, however, we have producers. Their objective is to maximize profit. Profit consists of two elements, revenue and cost. Revenue is the amount of money earned by producers from the sale of goods and services. Costs are the expenses associated with running a business: rent, electricity, salaries, etc. In order to increase profit, a producer would increase revenue, or decrease cost, or some combination of those two procedures.

I then tell my classes the story of the first Thanksgiving Kelly and I spent together as a married couple. We spent this time with her family in Hiram, Georgia. We had a huge feast on Thursday evening, and I went to bed in a near comatose state. I slept well that night. I vaguely remember drooling on my pillow so much that I flipped it over in order to enter into the next phase of sleep. All of a sudden, prior to 5 AM my new bride jumped out of bed like she was being shot at. She left the house almost immediately. No coffee, no make-up, no nothing, just left. And she was gone all day!

You know what she was doing, right? She was shopping. This is the day we call "Black

Friday." Contrary to some, it did not come by this moniker from shoppers becoming black and blue fighting over great deals on consumer goods. It is called "Black Friday" because it begins that amazing time in the world of retail where producers move from loss to profitability. To use an accounting term, the move from the "red" into the "black."

For me, the most intriguing part about this day and those ensuing is that both sectors of the economy are excited at the same time. Consumers are happy because they are maximizing satisfaction by getting great deals. We feel we are paying less and getting more in return. Businesses are excited because most of them generate more revenue in these few weeks, than in the six months prior! It's a win-win. Both sides feel like they're getting a great deal!

Do you know who else gets a great deal? Those people who choose to put their trust in Jesus Christ, the Son of the Living God. Mark 8:37 asks, "What can a man give in *exchange* for his soul" (*emphasis added*)? As a Christ follower, we trade our sin for His righteousness. We trade our righteousness, which is as filthy rags (Isaiah 64:6), for His holiness. We trade our poverty for His riches (2 Corinthians 8:9). We trade places, and

He received the wrath of God for our sins that is due us (Galatians 1:4 & Ephesians 5:2). What a great deal! Now that's worth getting up early for!

Here Comes the Bride

(**I** cannot believe I'm about to start a chapter in this book with this sentence.) The other day I was watching The Learning Channel's (TLC) reality show "Say Yes to the Dress." In my defense, I'd just come home from riding horses (that's a very manly activity, right?), and my wife already had it on the T.V. (I know, I know, "Sure, Justin. Whatever you say. We know you watch it ALL the time.") I do admit, however, that it was me and not my wife that picked up the remote and pressed the "pause" button so that I could contemplate what I was seeing and hearing.

For those who have never seen the show (bless you for your purity), it's basically a "reality" show that follows brides-to-be seeking the perfect wedding dress in the premier bridal salon, Kleinfeld in Manhattan. You can imagine the drama that unfolds on any episode as drama queens, stage moms, mother-in-laws-to-be, and grooms in waiting use passive-aggressive, or very aggressive tactics to get their way. It is indeed a train wreck that might be difficult to turn away from.

As I made my way through the living room pretty much oblivious to the television (stop snickering), I overheard a consultant asking the bride-to-be what she was looking for in a wedding dress. The woman's response was "Trashy." Insert clip here of consultant in an interview obviously recorded later, "I've had brides say in response to that question, "edgy" or "over the top" or even "gaudy," but never "trashy".

Why? Why would a bride ever want to look trashy on her wedding day? Well, quite honestly, I don't know. I could offer a guess about this woman's family background, self esteem issues, or the persona she wants to project, but that would be total conjecture. The real question I want to ask is "Are you a trashy bride?"

I love my bride. I think she is an amazing woman. I even call her "The Amazing Kelly" sometimes. You can talk bad about this broken down, bent-over redneck all you want to. I'll even let you get away with talking bad about my snot nosed kids, a little bit. But talk bad about my bride, talk bad about Kelly, then we've got problems.

Many times throughout scripture, the church is referred to as Jesus' bride. Revelation chapters 19-21 is the picture of a wedding ceremony between Jesus Christ the bridegroom and we, the church, his bride. Ephesians 5:25-27 reads, "Husbands, love your wives, just as Christ loved the church and gave himself up for her *to make her holy, cleansing her* by the washing with water through the word, and *to present her to himself as a radiant church, without stain or wrinkle or any other blemish, but holy and blameless."* (*emphasis added*). Doesn't sound trashy to me.

Listen to Chip Ingram's thoughts on this subject as related in "Living on the Edge":

In our efforts to...become relevant to "the culture," it appears we have fallen into it. I fear we have become a generation of Christians convinced that sex, salary, and status are the real keys to a life of fulfillment and happiness. The average believer, according to research, does not live in any appreciably different way from those outside of Christ. The culture's promises...have resulted in unprecedented divorce, financial collapse, disenfranchised children...

The church of the twenty-first century is weak and worldly...At the heart of "worldliness" is who you love and who you trust to meet the deepest needs of your life...If we would begin to feel deeply sad about running into the arms of (this other) lover (called "the world"), and comprehend how deeply this grieves our God who loves us and longs to give us the best, I think we would see a lot more Christians living like Christians (p.66).

In the fourth chapter of James, the Bible says that anyone who chooses to be a friend of the world becomes an *enemy* of God. There's an old country song that says, "I like my women just a little on the trashy side." Maybe so...but God doesn't.

The Dream

I am not a song writer, and after reading the following, you'll say "Amen" to that. But many moons ago this little tune stuck in my head, and I decided to write it down. While I was growing up, my Dad always listened to country music, except, of course, on Sunday mornings. Then the radio station he always listened to played Southern Gospel music. While we ate breakfast and got ready for church, we listened to the sounds of the Kingsmen, Gold City, the Bishops, the McKamey's, and the like. While no one in my house ever said that Jesus himself listened to Southern Gospel music, it was pretty much understood. While I no longer believe that, this song is in tribute to those groups. Imagine one of them singing this song, or better yet, imagine the crowd clapping on 1 and 3 as it's sung to the tune of the old Ray Steven's classic, "Would Jesus Wear a Rolex on His Television Show?"

I dreamed I went to Heaven last night,
I rolled up to those pearly gates.
There I met Saint Peter,
But He said, "Son you'll have to wait."
He went and got a tape measure,
Checked my chair from side to side.
He said, "Man, you can't get through the door
'Cause your wheelchair's just too wide.'

179

Now I've read in the Bible.
I know what it has to say
About straight being the path to Heaven
And narrow being the way.
Then Jesus He came on the scene
And He took me by the hand.
He said, "Son you don't need that chair no more
'Cause you can freely stand.
Chorus:
And I went walking into Heaven that day
Me and Jesus were arm and arm.
He gave me the grand tour of glory.
He showed me its splendor and all of its charm.
I got a brand new body.
It wasn't bent, or broken, or scarred.
And they towed that wheelchair away
Like an illegally parked car!

Jesus said, "Politically correct folks
Want to talk about accessibility.
They say Jesus, when are you going to put ramps
in here?
And where are all the good parking spaces going
to be?"

He said, "I am the Great Physician
If I know one thing it's how to heal.
So you won't need a cane or crutches
And you sure don't need those wheels!"

Repeat Chorus
Big Finish:
And they towed that wheelchair away
Like an illegally parked car!

www.annalwightphotogrpahy.com

ABOUT THE AUTHOR

Justin earned both his Bachelor's and Master's Degrees in Agricultural Economics from Mississippi State University. He has been employed in post-secondary education for more than twelve years. His current position is Economics Instructor at Jefferson State Community College, where in 2004 he received the Phi Theta Kappa Outstanding Faculty Member Award, and in 2008 was nominated for the college's Outstanding Faculty Member Award. Justin served on the Board of Directors for Special Equestrians, Incorporated, a therapeutic horseback riding facility. Through the years, Justin has taught small groups, spoke at youth meetings and given motivational speeches. He and Kelly, his wife of four years, are members of Valleydale Church, in Birmingham, Alabama, where they serve in the children's ministry as well as in a leadership role in their Life Connection Group. They reside in Moody, Alabama and are the proud parents of two children, Will and Anna Morgan.

For booking information, contact justfish419@yahoo.com .

Made in the USA
Lexington, KY
19 September 2019